T0285950

"Through a powerful combination of mindset, passion, good habits, hard work, and character, Don Ha has written a powerful book that will allow you to achieve exponential success. Truly having balanced success in every area of your life requires all of these things, and Don's life story is a testimony to this. If you are ready to think bigger and achieve incredible success, then I strongly recommend you start reading *The Art of Exponential Success* today!"

—TOM ZIGLAR

CEO, The Zig Ziglar Corporation

"Don's book is an extraordinary gift to the world. It left me feeling profoundly inspired to unlock the full potential of my life, instilling not just a desire to achieve more but also an unshakeable belief that I am capable of doing so.

Like many of the children I have met in my time at UNICEF, Don faced incredible adversity in his early years. Through his captivating storytelling, he vividly portrays the power of the human spirit to overcome immense hardship and highlights the potential each child harbors despite their circumstances.

What sets this book apart is Don's balance between inspiration and the practical. He bares his heart with warmth and unwavering determination, leaving readers feeling uplifted and motivated. With each turn of the page, he encourages us to think big while providing invaluable advice that paves the path toward achieving our lifetime goals.

The Art of Exponential Success is a true gem fit for leaders, teachers, parents, and students alike. Don's humble leadership and spirit of servanthood set a powerful example, destined to inspire countless generations to come."

—MICHELLE SHARP

CEO, UNICEF Aotearoa, New Zealand

"*The Art of Exponential Success* is more than a business book about making money. It is a book about transforming adversity into success. It's about evaluating and defining the life you desire. It's about personal growth, introspection, compassion, and giving back.

'Success' defined by Don is not merely about money. He acknowledges that money is a result of success but that personal accomplishment and being able to give back to family and community is the greater definition of success.

Don found success in the real estate industry through hard work, extra hours, and a lot of effort, but he will attest that his exponential success was achieved through his journey of transformation, pushing past barriers, and breaking through his limiting beliefs.

Don shares the secret for the foundation of his sales and success: trust. And this secret along with his many other thought-provoking concepts will encourage and motivate you to self-reflect. Don's story will encourage you to dream bigger, to revisit your past for inspiration, and to never forget where you came from."

—SHAWNA GILBERT

Senior Vice President, RE/MAX Global and Commercial

"Regardless of your identity, this book radiates hope—a hope centered on forging a future surpassing your past. It serves as an inspiration to envision grand and brilliant prospects, regardless of how challenging or limited your life may have seemed until now. Its relevance spans across all individuals, anywhere, who yearn for improvement in their lives.

This book is designed for all individuals from all walks of life who aspire to shift their lives from obscurity to achieving the status of a successful brighter future and breaking the cycle of generational poverty."

—TOM PANOS
Australasia's #1 Real Estate Coach

The Art of Exponential Success is an absolute game-changer. Inspiring, authentic, and practical, this book is a must-read for anyone wanting to transform their lives and create massive success."

—ROBIN BANKS
International Speaker and Mind Power Expert

THE ART OF
EXPONENTIAL
SUCCESS

THE ART OF

DON HA

EXPONENTIAL SUCCESS

HOW LITTLE STEPS, BIG DISCIPLINE, AND BOUNDLESS COMPASSION CAN TRANSFORM YOUR LIFE

Forbes | Books

Published by Forbes Books, Charleston, South Carolina.
An imprint of Advantage Media Group.

Forbes Books is a registered trademark, and the Forbes Books colophon is a trademark of Forbes Media, LLC.

Printed in the United States of America.

10 9 8 7 6 5 4 3 2 1

ISBN: 979-8-88750-107-9 (Hardcover)
ISBN: 979-8-88750-108-6 (eBook)

Library of Congress Control Number: 2023921590

Cover and layout design by Lance Buckley

This custom publication is intended to provide accurate information and the opinions of the author in regard to the subject matter covered. It is sold with the understanding that the publisher, Forbes Books, is not engaged in rendering legal, financial, or professional services of any kind. If legal advice or other expert assistance is required, the reader is advised to seek the services of a competent professional.

Since 1917, Forbes has remained steadfast in its mission to serve as the defining voice of entrepreneurial capitalism. Forbes Books, launched in 2016 through a partnership with Advantage Media, furthers that aim by helping business and thought leaders bring their stories, passion, and knowledge to the forefront in custom books. Opinions expressed by Forbes Books authors are their own. To be considered for publication, please visit books.Forbes.com.

This book is a tribute to my parents and my family for their unconditional support throughout my career. To all my friends, colleagues, and clients throughout my journey, you have provided me with unconditional support and guidance, enabling me to learn from each one of you and integrate your experiences into my successful career. This book would not have been possible without the support of each of you, regardless of how small or significant your contributions have been. I sincerely thank you, and this book is dedicated to you.

—Don Ha

*He who wants to succeed should learn
how to fight, to strive, and to suffer.
You can acquire a lot in life if you are
prepared to give up a lot to get it.*

—BRUCE LEE

CONTENTS

INTRODUCTION

To hell with circumstances; I create opportunities.

—BRUCE LEE

As a keynote speaker on stage, miked in front of a thousand people, the trickery of acoustics caused me to hear my own echo—just a snippet of my voice reverberating back to me as I gave my speech. I looked out at the crowd in the massive ballroom, glittering under a majestic crystal chandelier, and I wondered if the echoes coming back to me could ever tell the full story.

I was speaking as an international leader in real estate—someone who routinely breaks records, only to set new goals and reach and surpass them again. I've sold *billions* of dollars of real estate. One of my biggest achievements was in 2009 just after the global financial crisis (GFC). One of my Singaporean developers trusted my experience and knowledge, so he appointed me to be in charge of the whole project from sourcing, financing, designing, and marketing the $80 million-plus Sunline Estate, the largest single-level housing development in South Auckland. Today its value would be $200 million plus the trust my vendor placed in me and my team. This has allowed him to travel between New Zealand and Singapore, and most of our contracts are done by emails. I've built on my strengths and am now the owner and CEO of RE/MAX New Zealand and Fiji; I am also a sought-after sales trainer, wealth mentor, and founder and director of Top One Real Estate 2015 Limited, trading as RE/MAX Revolution.

Perhaps, most important, I have impacted countless lives. I have mentored hundreds and hundreds of investors to build wealth through property investing, as well as other business models. I've made everyone in my family, as well as many clients, and young couples and families whom I have guided, into multimillionaires. I have offered the protective wing and guidance of my experience to people who have come to me for my advice and wisdom.

But what the audience in that ballroom could not know was where I started and what it took to get me where I am. More than that, I wanted to convey to them what I now know from my extraordinary experiences, and how they, too, could transform their lives.

The man standing before them, ready to speak of success principles and his meteoric rise in the real estate industry in New Zealand, was once a refugee child living in a building in the shadow of five-star hotels, convention centers, and street-side markets overflowing with tourists from the West near Dundas Street. There, on probably the most dream-filled stretch of real estate in Hong Kong, is where my family had escaped to from Vietnam.

How could a ballroom full of people in their finest clothes, eating a spectacular meal, understand being ten years old and selling discarded tins of food to survive, or sleeping on a concrete floor and in apartment building lifts, with my entire large family in a single room? These are things that I can never forget, nor would I want to—because those experiences helped to make me who I am. Those experiences also taught me that one of my missions in life is to help those around me to rise from their circumstances, whatever they are.

My family eventually was granted refugee status to come to New Zealand. At that time, I had never even heard of such a place. In fact, until we left Vietnam for Hong Kong in a desperate bid for freedom, peace, and safety, I had never even seen a Caucasian person. I remember looking at a map and seeing that New Zealand was surrounded by a vast blue ocean. To a boy who felt so unsettled by his family's flight from the only world he had ever known, scarred by the dire circumstances, all he could think was, *If we have to leave our home again, where would we go—and with all that ocean, how would we get there?*

Years later, in my teens, I used to drive my old, beat-up minicar with my school friends up to the highest points on the cliffs of my adopted country of New Zealand. At the tops of these vast hills were the mansions of the wealthy in the affluent suburb of Saint Heliers in Auckland, with its views of the volcanic Rangitoto Island. These mansions and homes were usually spectacular structures with windows designed to showcase their vantage point. Auckland uniquely has Manukau Harbour on the Tasman Sea and the Waitematā Harbour on the Pacific Ocean, a place of rare beauty. The water is a deep and calming blue. I remember thinking, *These people in these million-dollar houses … what is it they do for a living? How could they possibly afford to live in such a beautiful home? What are their families and children like?*

Now I own the highest home on the cliff in that very suburb with unobstructed views that never fail to amaze. I often walk past the place I used to park my car in my teenage days and look up to my now family home and tell my children my story.

So, how did the boy who used to sell dented tins of food to survive in Hong Kong come to sell billions of dollars of real estate and control billions of dollars of development New Zealand-wide on behalf of these developers and others? And how is it that, unlike some, I have never forgotten where I came from and all I lived through? Part of it is hard work and never giving up—but also always ensuring

I offer a helping hand to others. I consequently am committed to transforming the lives of the people who cross my path, whether those people work with me or are anxious first-time homebuyers. I've elevated the RE/MAX brand nationwide in New Zealand.

When I finished my speech in that ballroom, I received a standing ovation. While that was wonderful, it was the people afterward who told me they were inspired to pursue unlimited success because of my words that made that moment all the more powerful to me. That was when I realized that I had a book within me that could reach still more people. In fact, during my initial years in real estate, I visited an elderly woman who was a numerologist. She asked if she could read my palm, and she told me that one day I would be writing books and teaching people as I have great leadership skills in me. At the time I just said yes out of respect for her, but in my mind, I thought because of her old age, she was just being nice to me. But look at me today … she was right.

As I talked to the people around me who waited for the opportunity to connect with me, I started thinking of what I could offer them—what wisdom I could pass along. I realized that I most desired for them to understand a few principles:

- Success cannot be confined. No-limits thinking is essential. If I made a million dollars one year, the next I planned how to make two. In one particular year, I challenged myself to make $1 million per month. Then in one particular seven-day period, I actually achieved earning $1 million that week. My next challenge is to consistently make $1 million a week, and I know my time will come.

- Small steps and changes can lead to big results. The point is to have a plan and *get started.*

- Big discipline! If I can get to the highest house on the cliff—one of the affluent areas with amazing views—after arriving in a strange country unable to speak the language, and have achieved, through hard work and discipline, millionaire status many times over, you can too.

- Cultivate boundless compassion. Without it, what are you working so hard for? Who are you sharing it with? And how can you help others along the way?

The Art of Exponential Success: How Little Steps, Big Discipline, and Boundless Compassion Can Transform Your Life is different from other books on success. I don't speak in metaphors and parables. I speak in real-life experiences. Every story in here is the truth, and I don't shy away from the difficult times (such as losing much of my wealth in the GFC of 2008, which I then had to earn back) as well as those "peak" moments (such as giving my speeches—or winning sales awards).

I don't think there is a finite amount of success to go around. The economy cycles—especially real estate. Sometimes it's a buyer's market; sometimes it's a seller's market. However, people tend to react with *fear* in times of uncertainty. Yet if you follow my steps and ideas, you will see that fear during uncertainty is reacting to the "sky is falling, the sky is falling" mentality, which is about *lack*. I know what it is like to feel such uncertainty, as you will learn in chapter 1. Being a refugee is humbling, frightening, and filled with distress and worry.

However, in this book, you will learn how I shed my "refugee" mentality—which is also about lack and fear—and instead embraced the idea of exponential success. From there, I entered the real estate business—despite nearly everyone around me telling me I could not do it. I not only proved the naysayers wrong, but I also surpassed every expectation the world had for me. Except my own expectation—because I *knew* that with discipline, hard work, the trust of the people you work with, and more, there are no limits.

As you begin to read this book and start to build wealth, I'll also explain how to *grow* it and *keep* it. (And if you *do* lose wealth or take a few steps backward, I will show you how to overcome any negative mindset—remember, if you built a fortune once, you can do it again.)

Finally, I will tell you this: I have helped so many buyers get into their first house, and then buy another and another to expand their real estate portfolio into millionaire status and more, that I joke I could walk from one end of New Zealand to the other and always have a place to stay and everyone would now welcome me to stay as I have helped them so much to where they are today.

Now, to be honest, New Zealand is over 260,000 square kilometers. So maybe *not quite* the entire country. But I very truthfully know that helping people get into their first real estate purchase is transformative, and it changes lives. *That* is as exciting to me as deals worth tens of millions of dollars.

So, join me as I reveal the secrets that have taken me from rags to riches, from fear and lack to selling a billion dollars of real estate and control of multibillions of dollars of real estate around the country and the world. Consider me your mentor as you aim for *exponential success.*

PART I
RAGS

C H A P T E R   1

REFUGEE

Talent is cheaper than table salt. What separates the talented individual from the successful one is a lot of hard work.

—STEPHEN KING

Where you are from and what you have been through shape you, for good or bad. Sometimes, we can even feel shackled to our pasts. But there are the brave few who unchain themselves.

My father, Khai Nguyen Ha, had experienced enough war, conflict, and tensions for several lifetimes. US planes had bombed his village in Vietnam and had killed whole families. He had been one of many men who had dug through rubble to find the bodies of small children and their mothers and grandparents smothered under the vestiges of what had once been their home. Those sorts of traumatic experiences color your whole existence. They are the types of memories that can keep us awake at night and can spring to our mind in quiet moments. I know my father longed for peace, for safety for his own family.

After the chaotic fall of Saigon and other crises, my father recognized that he was no safer than when the Americans were bombing. As a Chinese-born man in Vietnam, despite being well respected in a high position in his town, he and his wife and children would face persecution. Vietnam is now a thriving country that trades with global partners, a place of magnificent food and culture and a country of great beauty. But wartime is brutal, no matter who you are, and war tears apart countries and cultures until they put themselves back together again.

The neighbors often came to my family's home to harass and bring unease to our family. They used to tell my mother, Thi Vy, that she could stay in Vietnam because she was Vietnamese, but the rest of the family had to go. Of course, she never considered separating from her family, but this campaign of intimidation took a toll.

For me, just ten, I knew on some level that we were barely existing. We weren't really *living*. My parents, clearly, had great weight upon their shoulders. Their eyes always held a look of worry. Though, like parents the world over, they often tried to hide the difficult circumstances we faced in whispered conversations, I could see it etched indelibly on their faces. In Vietnam, my father would never really be trusted because he was Chinese-born. Our predicament was so serious that my father instructed us not to drink from the urn at our school because he was afraid we might be poisoned.

Facing the uncertainty of his situation in Vietnam, not seeing a future there, my father courageously decided to take my mother and six of us siblings (one of my older sisters was unable to join us at first because of having a newborn) and escape. He and his brothers began to build a boat big enough for thirty people. This had to be done under absolute secrecy in the dark of night. Had they been caught, my father would have been imprisoned or worse.

However, before he could launch his boat, an opportunity came for him. Two of my uncles, both of whom had served in the army and possessed navigational skills, were offered a large boat capable of accommodating up to two hundred people. The condition for our entire family to have a free passage to Hong Kong was that they would be in charge of navigating the boat through China.

In twenty-four hours, the decision was made. There would be no looking back. In the space of a day, we gathered a few belongings and left all we had ever known. Isn't that sometimes how life is? It can change in a moment, in a blink, and by a single choice that ripples through your life like the rings surrounding a tossed pebble in the still waters of a pond. I often think back, *Could I even do it now, with my family?* Yet, somehow, as a boy, I did.

When we boarded that boat, all my parents had was a dream of a better life. And that's all it was—a dream. They had no money. There were no guarantees for what lay ahead. We slept on the floor of the boat's hold, a cacophony of desperate people all longing for a life free from the threat of war and harassment, a life of future opportunity.

Though my father is very reserved, and we are very different, I admire his courage. So many of us fear our dreams, sometimes to the point of paralysis. We cannot move forward, and what is behind us is no longer. So, we remain very stuck. Though my family had an extreme experience, we must realize that dreams, big and small, can take us out of our comfort zones. However, as you'll see in this book, if your ambitions don't scare you, you aren't dreaming *big* enough.

In Hong Kong, life was quite difficult, requiring each of us in our family to carry our share of the very hard work it took to keep us minimally fed, clothed, and safe as we waited for our application for refugee status and placement to be processed. My father was persevering as well as clever. Once he was approved to work, he took jobs in construction—but then hired his own work crews and expanded his operations, showing an entrepreneurial streak.

For my part, our family longed for the food of our homeland. We were given items we had never eaten—baked beans, spaghetti (cheap starches), and so on. I would collect dented tins and cans and sell them for $2 each. I guess this is where my sales skills developed at the age of ten. Then I would take that money and go to the market to buy fresh vegetables and whatever we could afford. I would take that home to my mother for her to cook us fresh, *familiar* food to the best of her abilities in our cramped circumstances. That touch of home, a reminder of who we were and where we were from, brought us comfort. Not just to our bellies but also to our hearts and souls. My siblings also took on odd jobs and duties to try to help us better our situation.

However, even with all our efforts, it was a struggle. We were given a room in an apartment complex for refugees and little else. There was no welcoming us with open arms. In fact, it seemed the world wanted to get rid of us.

We still see that today in the tragedies of refugees the world over.

The United States was our first choice of where we wanted to settle. The world over tends to think of the United States as the land of opportunity—the American dream. England was our second choice, then Canada, and finally Australia. But the refugee quota for entry into those countries was full. Overflowing, in fact, from the displacement of war and humans' inhumanity to humans.

Eventually, we were told that New Zealand was accepting refugees. I had never even *heard* of this country, and I knew it was far, far away. However, eventually after two long years in Hong Kong, we were on to the next leg of our extraordinary life journey on a plane—my first time on one.

The Mangere Refugee Resettlement Centre in South Auckland was a different situation from the one we had inhabited in Hong Kong. For starters, we were welcomed. Our family had a sponsor from a local church. Members of the congregation would visit us in

Mangere, ensuring our stocks of food never ran out. Extra blankets were asked for and received as well.

One of the first things I noticed in the refugee center was that my family and I were now a minority. We had only ever been around Asian people. But all of a sudden, we were now sharing our temporary living location with Europeans and Polynesians. In our little town in Vietnam, we had not owned a television—our world was in that small place. All these people and places were unfamiliar. We had, after all, moved somewhere nearly nine thousand kilometers away.

I was a twelve-year-old boy and very impressionable, and the events we all lived through are seared into my brain. I remember at the refugee camp there were also a few Russians. One day, in the cafeteria that we all shared, this massive Russian man started to walk purposefully toward me. I was panicking. The only other Europeans that I had ever seen were the occasional policemen in Hong Kong. As he got closer to me, I was trying to figure out what I should do—I was this little kid, and this man seemed to block the sun, as his shoulders were so big. He reached into his pocket and gave me a lollipop. That was my first experience of interacting with a European.

Eventually, we settled into South Auckland, in a house we qualified for through the state. Every time we ventured into the city of Auckland, to me we might as well have been visiting Mars. It was overwhelming to be around the noise and hustle and bustle. We all struggled to adapt to life in New Zealand. Not to mention to learn the language.

With just the most basic English (mainly a few phrases), communicating with my classmates in my new school was difficult. It made for some lonely times. I had mastered "Fine, thank you," as one phrase, and I gave that response to pretty much any question I was asked.

I was quiet, but inside I was tough. (After all, look at all I had already experienced as a child. No carefree memories for me!) The kids bullied me for my broken English, but frankly, as a refugee, I was used to people looking down on me and my family. It was the same terrible attitudes toward us in different locations. I did not let it faze me. They would singsong tease me and call me "Ching Chong." I ignored it. But, in my own parenting all these years later, I have always encouraged my children to be accepting and welcoming to all.

Some kids eventually took to me because they felt sorry for me, I think. I figured out pretty quickly who were the good kids and who were the bullies to avoid. And, for some reason, I always ended up hanging around with the "bad" kids—the ones who didn't mind causing a little trouble. I never actually did bad things, but they were happy to have me around. I became a de facto leader. I'd be the one coming up with suggestions. *You go and do that* … I don't know what it was, but even though I could hardly speak English, these kids—the bad ones—looked up to me. They weren't allowed inside our house— they had to wait outside because my father didn't trust them. After a few years of going to school with the same people, they were finally allowed in the garage!

In a way, not having other Asian families around us was a godsend, because we didn't have the option of migrating toward other Asian families, where we would feel most comfortable and familiar. Instead, we had to mix with kids we attended school with and other families in the community. I can see now, as I travel to other countries and meet all sorts of people and personalities, even if we are very different, I can find our commonality and humanity.

While I was finding my way in the New Zealand school system, my father got a job with some other Vietnamese people in the boiler room at the DB Brewery in Otahuhu. He was paid $120 a week for a very hot, challenging job—but one he could perform even with no English skills. If bottles fell over going through the conveyor belt, he and my uncles who worked there would stand them back up. The job required no English! However, as in many, if not most, refugee families, our family *all* worked and pooled our money. My adult siblings gave their pay to my father, all of us pooling our finances together. That allowed him to save and save. Within four years, we'd bought our first house in Papatoetoe for $54,000.

My father had a vision and a plan. Soon after, we had enough money to buy a bakery in Western Springs, which one of my brothers ran. Once he was at the bakery, I had to go and work for him. One bakery would eventually become twenty-four bakeries. By the time I went to work there, I'd been immersed in Kiwi culture for long enough to know that I was entitled to keep my money! The children and teens there were more modern in that way and did not think like refugees in the sense of all contributing to the household. I worked all weekend, every weekend. I also valued the money because it was the only cash I would get to go to the movies or to the video game parlor with my friends.

This refugee mindset where everyone works together to elevate the entire family is one I have often touted. Times have changed, and it's rarer that families collectively pool their money. But the idea that you can each help the other is one of the most positive traits I learned as a refugee. The power of working together and saving together supercharges your efforts to get ahead.

In addition, my entrepreneurial side was already developing. One weekend, I went to the Otara Markets and noticed that people were selling watercress. And one day, shortly after, I saw watercress in one of the local ponds and figured I could make some money. I'd harvest the watercress and then wholesale them to a veggie shop in Mangere every Wednesday morning. I found another client or two, so I was making

$400 a week just selling watercress. Then a supermarket contracted with me for watercress. Here I was, a skinny kid with just passable English skills, and I was providing this to a major grocery store chain.

Every Tuesday, my younger brother and I would go to the pond and cut up watercress bunches. One Tuesday, we arrived at the pond, and the council had cleaned it all up, and my $400-a-week worth of watercress was gone! It was probably for the better, because it was dangerous work—I didn't know how to swim. I'd only want to go knee deep, but to get the watercress, you had to go deeper. I threw a pallet out into the water and stood on it, but it was dangerous. If I'd fallen in, I would have drowned. I learned that first hard lesson—how I could lose my business through no fault of my own. But such lessons also taught me to find other ways to reinvent myself.

My next entrepreneurial venture was intertwined with a passion I discovered. I joined a martial arts class. And by the time of my Fifth Form year, I'd impressed my instructors so much that I was asked to take on one of the Kung Fu classes. I had to stand in front of the class and count to them as we did drills. The first time I did it, nothing came out of my mouth! I was too shy. When you have thirty students for a Kung Fu warm-up, you have to be heard. So that was probably the best thing that could have happened to me at that time. I got louder and louder. And as I got better at Kung Fu, I gained more confidence. People started to recognize my talent. So, even though I couldn't speak English perfectly, people in the class wanted to ask me questions and learn from me. By the time I graduated high school, I had trained roughly a thousand students. This was a blessing, too, as my black belt and training taught me to be fearless and taught me the art of humble leadership.

School was not a passion for me, and it was a struggle, but entrepreneurship was not. I continued to work for and with my family.

Then, always thinking big, I went and opened a nightclub with $30,000. This was one of those lessons we learn—from being young. Of course, I envisioned that owning a nightclub would be the best business in the world. Not only are you around the nightlife, music, and beautiful people, but, surely, nightclub owners make a lot of money as well.

However, I didn't have any licensing, no handicap toilet, no fire exit. I just went and opened it. After three months, the council shut me down (I can't say I blame them). I lost all my money, and I thought, *This is it. My life is at an end. I've got nothing left.*

But you will see from this story—and others I share—that in my eyes, giving up is never an option.

I went on to sell Kirby vacuum cleaners. I joined a multi-level marketing company. I thought I could parlay selling into a million-dollar career. I had a knack for it.

My father often told me that I would never earn fortune and wealth.

"You're always looking for million-dollar idea," he would tell me. He advised me instead to open a bakery with his assistant, and then he wanted me to continue—as was the family way—to give him all the money I earned until such time as I married and got my own house and a business.

However, I was always the rebellious son. I insisted that I would run the bakery myself—and keep what I earned. My father agreed—on one condition.

I would be *on my own.* And by that I mean he insisted that from that point on, I would need to walk my own path. He would no longer help me. I was an independent man.

At that moment, I felt as if I had been ousted from my family to survive in the wilderness. Despite that, I applied myself with intensity.

Bakeries are very grueling, tiring work. You can't sell old, stale cookies and bread. Every day you must rise before dawn, while it is still dark out, and prepare all the baking and perform all the work to be able to open that day with fresh goods, then selling all day, then cleaning up, and then prepping for the next day. Rise. Repeat.

I worked six days/seventy-two hours a week at a minimum. And I made about $30,000 or so a year.

I had a regular, meanwhile, who always came in seemingly happy each day, very well-dressed in expensive suits, driving a sports car. One morning as I handed him his order, I asked what he did. It turned out he was a real estate agent.

I viewed real estate at that time as an investment opportunity. I liked to visit real estate agencies on my own day off. I had bought my first home to rent out to tenants at the age of twenty-two—and was negotiating for my second. I had planned to keep adding to my portfolio.

However, this was an opportunity to ask more about the profession itself. The agent told me he earned a commission of about $12,000 or so for each house he sold. Now *this*, to a young man (twenty-three or so at the time), sounded like a great career. A no-limits career.

I had also started listening to Zig Ziglar. His mindset was that you commit to being "all in" on your dreams. So, next I did something that horrified my family and community.

I sold my bakery for half the market value (at a loss). And I embarked on a real estate sales career.

My mother cried, because she used to count my money every day when I brought it home from the bakery, because I was still living at our home. My father initially thought I was crazy and said, "You'll fail! Why would you do this? That is a career for European people. Not you."

My community was filled with naysayers. No one, quite literally no one *but me*, thought I would succeed.

Yet here I am with over a billion dollars of sales under my belt and counting.

In order to do that, I had to *reject* the other side of the refugee mindset. There is a cautious single-minded focus to the refugee community sometimes. I understand. People who have undergone experiences like my family's want what's "safe."

There is that fear of "what if." And it's never the positive mindset of "What if everything goes right and Don Ha is a huge success and makes a million dollars?" Instead, it is the "What if you fail? What if you lose everything?"

Now multiply my family's doubts in me by an entire community, and you have some idea of what I was up against. While there is a stereotype (often very true) that refugees are some of the hardest workers, there is also a "refugee" mindset that can hold you back. And you don't need to be a refugee to have that fear-based attitude. Too many of us think, "What if I lose it all?" instead of "What if I am hugely successful?"

So, what happened when I sold my bakery and decided to become a real estate agent despite all the voices around me telling me I would fail? All the voices, quite frankly, *rooting* for me to fail? Urging me to return to the safety of the community, of the expected path?

Well, that is the next step in our journey to exponential success.

It is time for chapter 2: Transformation!

TRANSFORMATION!

Your attitude, not your aptitude, will determine your altitude.

—ZIG ZIGLAR

In order to succeed, in order to transform your life, I will let you in on a secret. You must believe in yourself, and you must ignore the naysayers. Transformation isn't possible without self-belief and growth. And growth is not possible without hard work and challenging yourself. My life was about to be transformed. Actually, that is not quite true. *I* was about to transform my life—that's the more correct way to view it. Transforming your life is not about wishing on a star and waiting for "magic" or winning the lottery. Transformation is about figuring out what it will take to change your life—and determining in yourself that you will make the change.

As I said in chapter 1, I sold my bakery and was about to embark on the adventure of my adult life. For me, to earn $30,000 a year in my shop, I worked seventy hours a week. Seventy hours of hot work near ovens, rolling dough until my arms were weary, dealing with my employees, picking up their duties if they did not show up, unloading cartons and crates of supplies—backbreaking work.

That is one of the first things people discover about me—I am *not* afraid of long hours and hard work. Again, one of the positives of the refugee experience for me and for my family was learning that hard work and sacrifice are part of our life experiences. Some people might call it "hustle." When you are a refugee, nothing—not even a homeland—is handed to you. In fact, much is taken from you: your home, your dignity at times, your sense of security and safety.

Worse, when you are a refugee, events and circumstances happen *to* you, things that are out of your control. Think about it—my father and mother and all the people of their generation—not to mention my siblings and me—did not start a war. But we had to deal with the consequences of one.

It is easy to stay in that mindset, but instead I wanted to break free and control my own destiny. The challenge of it all was exciting, and business seemed to run through my veins, whether that was collecting watercress or learning the real estate business.

Even though I was proud to own my bakery, there had to be a much better way to carve out my path to success—a way that ignited a passion in me. I was making a living—it was stable and secure. But security can also be stifling because it does not always encourage growth and innovation. In addition, it was chosen *for* me—not *by* me. But real estate was different.

Perhaps it was the answer then to an unstated prayer or dream that I encountered that well-dressed real estate agent in my shop. I could mentally calculate the math—if I sold three houses at what he said he made per house, I would surpass my current wages. If I sold five, I could double my current situation.

I already owned my first home, which I had bought for $42,000. I had a mortgage debt of $20,000. Now at the age of twenty-two, I had a new title to my name—I was a landlord. Even that, to my community, was not a positive achievement. Rather than applauding a young man moving into property investing, the Vietnamese culture, as a whole, does not believe in debt. In fact, at the time, I had a Vietnamese girlfriend, and she left me because I had a mortgage. I am sure she may kick herself now when she sees my smiling face on a billboard or my name on a building.

On Mondays, my day off from the bakery, I used to be obsessed with real estate. I would drive around, looking at properties and communities, learning all I could. I was smart enough to know that real estate was a sound investment as long as you know what you are doing—or have someone like me who is trustworthy and can advise you ethically. (You will see in this book that trust and integrity are nonnegotiable with me.)

I was looking at real estate to purchase a second home as an investment/rental income. Walking into various real estate agencies, if they had a listing for $50,000, I offered $25,000. I knew it was highly unlikely I would get those houses at such a lowball price. I never did end up buying one. Nonetheless, what it did for me was to give me the practice run of how to negotiate and how to work out an offer. I could assess how good the agent was—what was their negotiating style? What was their sales pitch? It taught me about service. It was better than any college class on real estate—I was gaining real-life skills and observations. As you will see in chapter 3, taking those small steps and learning from real-life experience is truly an education money cannot buy.

I also already knew I had a knack for sales. After all, how many *children* do you know negotiating with markets for watercress? As an adult, I had sold many products for a multi-level marketing company, and I had sponsored dozens of people to move up through the ranks quickly. As an organization, the multi-level marketing company had a very positive effect on my life. They take you under their wing and teach you. They give you a model or path to follow—and what is wonderful is they applaud all your successes. In fact, that sort of philosophy is one I apply at my real estate company because it's about paying it forward. I am happy to guide people new to the business, and I am willing to take on untested new agents if they are eager to learn and are motivated. I know what it is like to not speak English well or to seem like an unlikely candidate for sales, but I will give the chance to people if they are eager to learn.

I have been asked many times what my "secret" to sales is.

Trust.

I can walk into a room, and I can look at someone, and I *know* this person will end up talking to me, and I can warm the room up. I'm very friendly. I can understand what people need and want, and I'm very transparent in my personality. So, within the first five minutes, if you can earn people's trust and respect, regardless of whether they are rich or poor, regardless of race or nationality, regardless of what they do for a career, that is the magic. If you *really* want to change your life, which I hope you do (which is perhaps why you bought this book), your name is your legacy. Can people trust that name, trust you? If they feel they can, they will do business with you.

Around this time, I also took an insurance licensing test. This test demonstrated the test taker's level of salesmanship, so it was a source of pride that I passed with flying colors. I was offered a salaried job in an office in the city, but something held me back from taking it. I imagined real estate on one side of a scale and insurance sales on the other. Which had the greater weight? Which called to me? Real estate ended up being my choice. The reason was this new career would give me *unlimited potential*. Think about that— exponential success. No-limits thinking. I knew that the harder I worked, the more money I would make, and the more opportunity there would be. So that outweighed the stability of the insurance position in an office.

Because I had taken up Shaolin Kung Fu at an early age and had attained my black belt and then trained other students, helping thirty-five or so attain their black belts, I had a competitive edge as well. The training was so ingrained in me from my teenage years, a decade or more of mental and physical training, I had the confidence to knock on people's doors and talk to anyone. I was fearless. I had developed deep confidence. Now it was time to apply the skills and drive I had to my new career.

I looked around at the other real estate professionals at my first position. I examined their sales. I saw the income possibility—if someone worked forty or fifty hours a week. It stood to reason that if I worked longer and harder, I would make more money (and this proved to be true). I worked seventy-five hours a week, consistently.

I sold my first house in my first month, but I got paid only $750 for my commission—so it wasn't quite the $12,000 the real estate agent told me he made. First, it was not my listing, so I earned only 40 percent of the selling fee. Second, I was starting at the bottom—not with million-dollar listings in the Saint Heliers suburb. But I was on my way.

I remember looking at that first check and thinking, *Wow, this is so much money. All I had to do to make this money was talk!* After a life of hardship, of risking drowning by pulling up watercress, and after watching my family work so hard for what we had, this idea was magical. That is the power of transformation—seeing something in a whole new way. For me, money was now not about working harder and more hours in a stifling bakery kitchen but rather working harder and *smarter* by connecting with people and talking and, most important, as you will learn, listening. When you truly listen to another person, listen with a discerning mind and heart, you will hear both what they say and what is unsaid. And then you can help them.

I was unafraid of rejection. A no just meant the next door might be my yes, because sales is a numbers game. A no also meant I could assess what I did, how I did, and how I might improve (you will see in chapter 3 that I do this for my sales team as well—helping them to analyze their performance). For exponential success and transformation, every day, we need to improve and better ourselves.

The second month, I sold three more houses. Then I got paid $4,500, because those sales were more in value. In my life as a bakery owner, it took me three months to make $4,500. At this point, I could "see" my future. This is very important—because once you see possibility, there should be nothing holding you back.

Transformation is about being free from the control of limiting beliefs. I had been raised to "accept" the life my parents had laid out for me, how they saw my life unfolding. They are not risk-takers. This is completely understandable, and I say this with great empathy. When you live through the horrors of war, and when you are taken from all you have known, security is the most important thing on your mind, particularly if you have children and a family to support.

But I wanted to break free of that "safe" and accepting mindset. Now I teach other people how to break those chains controlling them too.

Here's a true story to demonstrate what I mean. Recently, a Vietnamese man came to me who had been in New Zealand for nearly three decades. He had asked for an appointment to see me, and when he came into my office, he was incredibly nervous. Anxiety was etched on his face, and I noticed his voice was shaky. When he came to our adopted country from Vietnam, he took work, as many immigrants do, in manual labor, as a painter. This is a fine profession if that is your passion, but in an instant, I could see right through him that his self-belief was so small that he thought he could *only* be a painter. As if real choice had been taken from him.

I asked him a few questions about his life and family to put him at ease. Most people, no matter how nervous, can answer questions about their own life. His wife was an accountant, and they had a couple of children. He confessed that he did not enjoy painting anymore because it was messy, difficult work, and as he was getting older, it bothered his back and shoulders. The physical side of his job was just getting to be too much.

He felt stuck, unsure of how to change and transform.

He owned a home (which he and his family lived in). This was a strong positive! It showed he could save and manage money. That is step number one. I remarked,

"Well, you have a house now, you know how to budget, and you've got some equity. Why don't you invest in some property for rental so that while you invest, your property makes money for you? In fact, your investment will make you more money than you can make painting. And then you can still continue painting for a couple more years as you grow your real estate portfolio. Once you make more money investing, you can quit painting or you can hire people in your painting company and earn less but be hands off."

I showed him some examples of clients who had followed my advice and done just that. However, I didn't think much about the conversation at the time because, in my many years of real estate, I have offered advice countless times—it does not mean people take it. Transformation will always be the marriage of opportunity, hard work, and *you*. Some people may find being in charge of their own destiny as opposed to working for someone else a bit scary. I think it's exhilarating.

About a week later, he texted me: "I really want to become an investor now, and I want to follow you, based on my meeting with you." I helped change his mindset within thirty minutes of meeting me (he initially only wanted five minutes, but I conversed with him for thirty). As the years have gone by, he has more than twenty properties and has fifteen staff working for him, running his painting business.

Here's another thing about transformation and self-belief. Often we put people in a box. We confine them to the four walls of the box—we overlook someone because maybe they have a different social status than we do, or have less education, or are from another country or belief system, whatever it is. However, perhaps even more critical to understand is that we sometimes put ourselves into the box. *We* do it, not others.

When starting out, perhaps the mindset is that successful people will not want to coach us. Sometimes, depending on culture, there can be other beliefs. An Asian refugee, for example, may want to meet a European mentor or businessperson they admire, thinking they have secrets to success. Or it may be they want to approach someone like me, who has sold billions in property and created many millionaires—but that leader (in whatever industry) will seem like they are from another planet, they are so out of reach. They will convince themselves that they cannot meet these people they look up to. They may not approach them or talk to them because they feel inferior.

And *that's* the biggest mindset they have to change.

Here is a secret: The more successful people are, the more inclined they are to help others starting out (at least, this is my mindset). They don't get any more kicks out of making money; they get more of a kick out of making people successful. And that's me. I get a kick out of helping others transform their lives, because their successes live in me, so that's my passion. It's sending out all that positivity into the world.

Yes, making money is a passion. Property development is a passion. Work is a passion. But truly, if you have $100 million in the bank, that's not inherently different from having $120 million in the bank. Money itself, for successful people, becomes a by-product. Money is a vehicle, if you will, for what you can do for others or for your family—or for other dreamers and strivers.

For me, I transformed my own life. So, my passion was then to transform my parents' lives, my siblings' lives, other people in my community's lives, and so on. Pay it forward (this is another theme you will see over and over in my life and in this book).

Consider also people like Jeff Bezos or Richard Branson. Space is a passion for these two men. After a while, what else are they going to do with their money? Philanthropy, yes. That's important. Caring for their families, sure, but they have done that many times over. But pursuing space? Their money is a vehicle—literally—to create rocket ships taking them and other private citizens into the stratosphere, which is an apropos metaphor.

When people are young and ambitious, they often say their goal is to be a millionaire (to fly toward the stratosphere). It's harder to become a millionaire now—inflation, cost of living, and so on. But it's still a goal for many. Making your first million is the hardest. You're usually learning your chosen business, and you are new at this millionaire pursuit. You're bound to make mistakes. Once you make that first million, the millions after that are still difficult to make, but you *know* you can do it. You did it once. You can replicate it.

I am sure you may have heard of the story of Roger Bannister, the English runner who broke the record for the sub-four-minute mile. If you are unfamiliar with that story, prior to 1954, no human had broken the four-minute mile, and the "mindset" of the world of sports and the world in general was that it simply could not be done. Humans just weren't made to run a mile in under four minutes. Since no one thought it could be done, the mentality pervaded the sport of track and field.

Until Bannister.

Since he broke that "barrier," thousands of more people have done so, too. So much so that you cannot be a world-class runner if you cannot run a four-minute mile.

What was *my* four-minute mile? Consider all the false or insecure mindsets and beliefs from my life that needed to be overcome:

- I did not speak English well.

- I was not born in New Zealand.

- I had no business connections at all.

- I did not have an advanced degree and, in fact, did not enjoy school.

- I had little to no experience in sales.

- I was a refugee.

- My family and community thought I was crazy for doing something with no "guarantee" or security.

- No one was showing me the way.

These are called "limiting beliefs." My first year in real estate I sold eighty-six homes. Eighty-six! And made nearly a half-million dollars. The average sales for a real estate agent in New Zealand at the time was one per month. I honestly don't know how I sold eighty-six properties in my first year.

Freed from my refugee mindset, the stratosphere was the limit.

Importantly, too, I announced my intentions to be a millionaire by age thirty. This was a rather audacious goal. My family was hard-working, but we had no frame of reference for that kind of success. Thus, here's another very important idea to keep in mind. Whatever it takes, if you are intent on transforming your life, go find yourself a mentor, go buy a book (like this one), and go listen to success speakers. If you do not have people around you to push you toward your goals, you will have to find your way. This is why I am always willing to mentor new people.

I will share a little story with you. Transformation is very much about evolving. Once you set on that pathway, others may not understand you. (There is a very real reason why the saying is "It's lonely at the top." Oftentimes, even the people closest to you may not comprehend your ambitions.)

Even today when I visit my parents, despite all the success I have enjoyed, rather than encouraging me to build more developments or pursue more goals, my father once said, "Why do you want to achieve so much? Why can't you be happy with what you have? I'm getting a headache, just watching you."

I replied, "You're getting a headache watching me because you don't understand how to solve the problems in my business. Where I don't get a headache because I can solve everybody's situation—real estate is my passion. Therefore, I never feel that stress."

My transformation also did not stop once I sold those first eighty-six houses, or once I made my first million. On November 14, 2005, I wrote down my next goal. I was worth about $10 million at the time. My stated goal was to be worth $100 million in assets by May 2008, with a net worth of $50 million.

I beat my goal by a year. In 2007, my total asset value was $117 million, and my net worth was $60 million.

Other goals included moving into my dream home in an affluent area—high up on the tallest vantage point overlooking the harbor, just as I had once dreamed. I also wanted to have three kids.

Checked off one goal. Then the next. Then the next. And on and on.

In terms of transformation, you absolutely must write your goals down. Once you write them down, you are responsible for them. You commit to them. If you want to be number one, you have to tell everyone about it. That creates the pressure to be number one. And that's a good pressure. It gives you motivation. If you set a goal and don't write it down and don't tell anyone, it's too easy to give up on it at the first sign of adversity.

And no one will know, and no one will hold you accountable— *including yourself.*

I'd look at that document where I wrote my goals every quarter or every six months. And as you achieve your goals, it fills you with even more confidence. I wrote down those goals because I am addicted to achievement. I am addicted to being what and who I want to be. At one point I wanted to own a hundred properties, so I went and bought a hundred clay houses and put them on my dining table so that I could visualize my goals. Needless to say, my wife was not happy with me, as when we had friends and family over, she would have to pack them all up. Today, I still have some of these house in my office, as I give them out to young aspiring investors.

If you want to transform your life, you need to work the hours. If you are going to only do forty hours each week, you won't make it in real estate. You need to do seventy hours a week for at least the first two years. That's the reality. I know that there is a glamorous perception of real estate agents—that you can sell a few houses and make millions. But there are no shortcuts in this industry. A new salesperson needs to agree to invest in themselves. A new salesperson needs to ensure they have good knowledge of the area they will be working in (study, study, study). A new salesperson needs to have good communication skills. They have to be prepared to help people. To go the extra mile. That makes you memorable and builds trust. This method will apply to any sales career.

Anyone can do it. That's what people don't realize. It's not a magic formula. It's the reality of what it takes, but you *can* do it. However, too many people walk into their interviews saying they want to be the next Don Ha. They think they can waltz in and duplicate my success—without the work. There will never be another Don Ha, precisely like me. But if someone truly aspires to be like me, they must understand it can happen only if they follow the principles of hard work, ethics, and sacrifices of time.

This is another truism. I personally know what it takes to transform your life. There is no favoritism in my world though. If a person wants to sell their house and they approach me, I will sell their house. I might be busy, but I will find time to do my job. If there is someone else struggling to make a sale in my office, I will make sure to take them with me so that I can provide them the knowledge, training, and tools for them to gain self-confidence to do the job themselves. Regardless of who it is in my office or team, whether it's my family or friends, there is no favor or special treatment. *Everyone* is entitled to the same opportunity to succeed.

To be Don Ha, you have to prepare to put in the hard yards and long hours in your first years of real estate and prepare to be ready for every sale and every question and study more. Be the most knowledgeable Realtor out there. Sometimes I look at newer Realtors, and I wonder if they are the type of people who will take the property paper home and read it three times each night so that they know the oppositions' stock and how many agents they have. I wonder if they are the type of people who will be able to match the pictures of houses to the street. I wonder if they will give up weekends to attend seminars. I wonder if they will want to work until midnight on a Tuesday and be the first one in the office on a Wednesday. Because if they want to be me, that's what they are going to have to do—not just day after day or week after week. They'll have to do it month after month for year after year.

I work longer than all of my staff. I'm in the office before most of them, and I leave after all of them. I know everything about my company. And I know my people. I think that's why they respect me. I'll get in the car with them and teach them how to go and do a cold call at a property. I give them the tools to transform their careers themselves. If one of my employees in the corner cubicle is a bit down, then I'll call him in and find out what's wrong. It's like a family—I know there is something wrong before they even tell me. That's how clued into my company I am.

The reality is every night before I go to bed, I will plan my next day. If I have a meeting with my staff in the morning, I will plan exactly what I want to say. If I want to play them a video clip or give them a passage from a book, I will go over things three or four times because I need to know the message. Even after all this time, I find myself rushing to go to work because I literally cannot wait to get there. Then when I'm at work, I don't want to leave. It's exciting. Exhilarating. But I have to be disciplined. I have a wife and three children waiting for me, so I have to go home and be the family man. But when I am at work, almost every thought throughout the day is about work. I think of it as going to war. We're fighting a battle, and we want to win. *Every day.* All of the senior people here feel the same about their jobs. They *want* to be here. If the agent doesn't have that feeling, they fail.

When you are a refugee in a strange new country, you have no option but to learn to work hard. You have to work hard initially not to thrive but to *catch up*. You have to learn a new language. Learn about a new culture. You are scrambling all of the time. But it teaches you the value of hard work. And the good news is you don't have to have a hard work ethic when you start working for me, because having a hard work ethic is something that you can learn. If someone gives me permission to, I'll teach them that work ethic. I will set them on the path to transformation.

Recently, a new salesperson started working for me, and one of her drives was to earn a lot of money. I told her that if she does the things I tell her to do, work the hours that I set out for her, make the sacrifices that I suggest to her, she can be a millionaire one day. She accepted the challenge, and I set out the steps for her to be successful. Of course, as I wrote previously, not everyone will follow through, but the majority of my staff will. To keep them motivated, I'll have regular meetings with them. Sometimes if I sense a little bit of a lull in someone, I will remind them of their goals. And I'll remind them that I have given them the recipe for success.

I know how to get to the mountaintop, so listen to me.

I always tell them to write their goals down. Not everyone wants to. So, I go to my filing cabinet and pull out that piece of paper. I show them that I *still* am setting goals, still evolving, still getting better at what I do.

Transformation is freeing. Sometimes, there is the temptation to only look forward. You've transformed, so why look over your shoulder at where you once were?

If I have a mantra, it is this: *Never forget where you come from.* It's not only a call to arms for humility but also to remind me that when the going gets tough, it's never as tough as the hopelessness that surrounded me like a dark fog as a child as I played in the gutters of Hong Kong.

In that sense I could be a poster child for Brent Taylor's 2007 book *The Outsider's Edge: The Making of Self-Made Billionaires*, which claims that the main element common among many self-made billionaires is an unhappy childhood.

My life experiences have taught me that nothing is too big of a challenge. Nothing is as scary as being on that boat leaving my home in Vietnam, not knowing what life had in store for me and my family. Consider the hardships you have been through. Perhaps they are not as dramatic as what my family and I endured, but we have all been through pain we had to overcome.

I have a policy that when I interview staff for both our commission positions and for salaried positions, because of my background, I always give them an opportunity. I am a refugee. I don't speak English properly. My first real estate boss helped me through my real estate course and gave me an opportunity. So, I like to give people the same opportunity. Regardless of their backgrounds, even if they have been in trouble with the law, if they have no outstanding warrants and they've paid their debt to society as set by the courts, then I'll give them a chance. It doesn't matter to me if people are poor. If they don't own a car, I'll give them a chance. It's funny; today when I hire someone, let's say with a colorful history, some of my existing staff will ask me why I hired them.

Just remember where you came from.

That's what I tell them. When you are successful, it's easy for you to forget your roots. The things I look for in people are drive and determination. That's what impresses me—not a fancy car or suit (though you will see in our next chapter that looking the part is important). They have to want to get out of the rut that they are in.

They have to want to *transform*. I'd prefer them to have integrity and honesty when they walk in for their interview. But if I sense that they don't, but I also sense they have the right levels of ambition, I'll take on the challenge to drill honesty and integrity into them.

Always, in my hiring process, if it comes down to two people and one is more qualified than the one with a bit of spirit about them, I'll almost always opt for the one with the fire in their belly.

People say that's a risk. Well, being in business is a risk. You can teach someone who is dishonest to be honest and to represent you in public. That's one of the greatest rewards. I believe I can help transform people. Over a six-month period, once they see and experience the culture that we have in my office, they want to become a better person. They want to embrace the culture—everyone is so positive and driven and welcoming. The rewards and results outweigh the risks. That's my experience. All we can do is give people an opportunity. It's up to them to take it.

It is up to them to *transform*.

We have situations too where we train people and, then, after we've put a lot of time and energy into them, they up and leave and take their newfound confidence somewhere else. One time, one of my staff left to open his own real estate company. He figured that after two years with me, he knew everything. He even convinced some of my staff to go with him. They failed. And I rehired them. That surprised a few people in the company, but I had to rehire them, because when the company failed, they were left with nothing. And to be honest, I admired him for having a go and trying to do it on his own. And I was quite proud of him, because he'd built himself up into a position where he had enough money to try something like that. If he'd been a failure here, he would never have had the money to try to set up his own company. There was reluctance from some staff to accept him back. Now he's best mates with everyone in the building again.

Never forget where you come from.

Many of the people who have shown up at my office for a job interview have been seduced by my rags-to-riches story—my transformation. They are, in many cases, unabashedly motivated by money alone. For some bosses, that would be off-putting. But not for me. Many of my staff say they want to be millionaires. Well, that's a piece of cake. It's easy—as long as you are prepared to commit to the things you need to do to make it happen. I can give you the recipe to making a million dollars. In fact, I can guarantee you that I will make you a millionaire. The only thing I need from you is commitment to your transformation.

In that sense, I have no problem with someone wanting to come and work for me, knowing that their main objective is to turn themselves into millionaires. Some people might see those people as selfish and accuse them of trading off the Don Ha name. I have no problem with their ambition, because it means they are motivated, and I see part of my role as making sure that they remain motivated. When they make it, if they want to leave and do something else, no problem. The way I see it is that I have given them their wings. They have transformed! If they want to fly here or somewhere else, do it. Just fly. Take advantage of the wealth you have acquired.

Not every member of my staff is motivated by wealth. For some, the personal motivation is just to have enough money to pay their bills and look after their family without stressing that there's "too much month and not enough paycheck," as they say. The overwhelming motivation though—from all of my staff—is the emotional payoff that comes when you help someone buy a house. To help someone get their finances sorted and to put the "Sold" sign on a property, that's the thrill. That's the kill. The *lead-up* to the payday is the thing that drives them.

Getting your commission is nice, but it truly doesn't compare with the thrill of putting someone into their first home or making a sale for a client who needed the sale to be made. Note that the subtitle of the book includes "boundless compassion." If you care about people and families and are seeing their joy when they find that dream home that will bring them happiness for years to come, that's the real reward.

Now, we'll look at the other piece of transformation—the steps you must take in order to completely change your life to one of exponential success.

CHAPTER 3

SMALL STEPS

> *The secret of getting ahead is getting started. The secret of getting started is breaking your complex overwhelming tasks into small manageable tasks and starting on the first one.*

— MARK TWAIN

We all learn to walk before we run. There are some people who are impatient, though. They want to run first and figure out how to walk later. Chances are they will fall down. Transformation is only possible through learning and changing bit by bit, with hard work, with small steps.

I presume you have seen the movie *The Wizard of Oz*. Dorothy and her friends' journey begins step by step on that yellow brick road. It is an arduous journey, full of challenges and danger, and in the end, Dorothy discovers the power that always resided within her. What better metaphor is there for our journey toward self-improvement?

Every story in this book is true—so let me share a powerful one that occurred during the global COVID-19 pandemic crisis. There is no person reading this book who was not affected by the virus—some of us far worse than others.

I was attending a Muslim wedding fairly early in the pandemic when people were still holding events. Because of the type of wedding it was, the men were on one side of the reception room and the women were on the other.

I saw a young man sitting alone, and I consider it one of my "superpowers" to befriend and talk to people. I take people from strangers to acquaintances to friends and colleagues. Since my wife was sitting on the opposite side of the room, I approached him and asked if I could sit with him. (Another success tip—always be networking, always be looking to make real connections with people!)

Making conversation, I asked, "What do you do for a living?"

He informed me he was out of work. "I was a manager at a duty-free shop, and because the airport closed, they've got no job for me." He shook his head. "I've actually got a double whammy. I want to be a pilot, and now I can't fly and continue my training."

I asked him how long he had been out of work, and he told me six months.

"What are you doing tomorrow?" I asked.

He replied that he was going job hunting. He had an interview for an hourly shift manager somewhere. I handed him my card and told him to come interview with me the next day. This is the type of thing I do sometimes—because I want to see the level of someone's motivation, the commitment in a person.

When he came to the office the next morning, I said, "I don't have a manager job for you, but I will give you a job. I'll pay you at minimum wage, and I want to see how quickly you learn."

I think I had an instinct that he was eager and willing to work very hard. Two years later, he's now earning more than what he earned at his previous job, *and* he's our national franchise sales manager with a level of respect from others. Exponential success is within his sights.

Soon after, employing my current national franchise sales manager, I was introduced to the company's now financial controller. During the interview process, I asked him, "What are you expecting in terms of pay?"

He replied, "I will accept the minimum pay and will prove my worth to you and the company." I was very impressed with his reply; this showed me he was willing to put in the hard work. He at first started under the wings of a senior team member, and when that leader later resigned, I asked if he was willing to take on her responsibilities. Again, he showed me his worth, that he was willing to learn and challenge himself. He has continuously proved his value and shown that with the correct leadership, anyone can grow and build legacies. Today he is the company's senior financial controller.

Too often, people think small, and they think short-term versus long-term. They want to be wealthy, but they want riches now. They may take a position that has a salary determined by someone else. That salary may be higher than starting in sales. But that job has a ceiling. The other does not. You may have to push through those two years of long hours and lower pay as you develop your network before you see big results, but in the end, those small and methodical steps can lead to exponential success with no limits.

It is a mistake to look at someone who is very successful and think they must have been born with a silver spoon in their mouth or assume it was always easy for them. When I first started initially, I was a salesperson. Granted, I was a salesperson who made nearly a half million dollars in my first year, but obviously from my story, you know I was not born to riches. I was very successful for ten years, and I had a small team with me. I did not try to run before I could walk. I learned and kept expanding and pursuing excellence step by step.

When the opportunity came for my own business, I took the leap—the big step at last, finally running. But I also knew I needed people with licensing and know-how to open the business. One of the biggest hurdles as you open your own business is creating your system—all of it. When you work under a company, that company has structures and systems.

When you go out on your own, you'll be saying, "How do I deal with complaints? How do I do this? How do I do that?" And that will be something that always set people back, that fear factor of having to establish all the aspects of a business. But, if you have great values in your business, great respect, and great staff respect, you can learn.

Now, in terms of small steps, what happens when you try to make a sale and it doesn't happen? Well, when you work with me, I'm going to help you—because so much of successful sales is preparation, preparation, preparation. Those small steps that add up to big success.

First, I will begin by asking the following questions:

- Did you turn up on time? Do not doom yourself to failure by making easily avoidable mistakes. There are setbacks that you have no control over. For example, perhaps the person who wanted to purchase the house had a change of heart because they want to live in a different neighborhood. There is no point in trying to talk someone into a house that is not right for them. But "unforced errors" are completely avoidable. Professionalism is nonnegotiable. Period.

- Did you bring a proper presentation with you? At my company, we always have brochures available along with other professional elements of a sale. Image is important. It helps the client build trust with you because they can see you know what you are doing and that the company is top-notch.

- When you studied your product, did you study the surrounding of the property? Did you study the comparable sales? Did you rehearse it? Practice makes perfect.

- Did you look the part? For any new entrepreneur at the start, they've got to have presentation skills. Meaning that they've got to dress up, and they must look successful and project that. If your hair is scruffy, well, get a haircut and shave yourself so you look like a businessman and you dress like one. If you are a woman, the same principle applies. Because if you look scruffy, you dress scruffy, your mind will be scruffy. It's called the Power of Appearance: look sharp, feel sharp, be sharp. Just like the Gilette contour ad.

And if none of the answers to those questions are yes, then we would certainly not give that real estate agent an A+. If you do not follow the system, then your failure is *yourself*, and you need to improve on that area. The good news is that means you have room to better yourself, to learn the small steps and the good habits that lead to exponential success.

Preparation is something that most people don't do. In fact, I think a lot of the failures people experience is because they aren't equipped for what they're working themselves into—for their goals. I equip myself way beforehand—I am always prepared. Even with all my success, I don't "wing it." Positive habits will never let you down.

Just imagine you are a pilot. You have a takeoff and landing checklist, and you rely on those to ensure you and your passengers' lives are safe.

These are the important lessons I try to convey. On a typical day, I actually don't sell houses. I mentor people more. I can't sell a house to one person every day, but say, in a typical month, I'll talk at three different events to two hundred people each. Then they all have the recipe for success. Then they go on and make sales, and it all exponentially multiplies. This is how you scale your business (which we will get into in the next part of the book). However, I will take a moment here to say that letting go and delegating are so important. You cannot grow exponentially to huge success unless you understand that you cannot clone yourself. At some point, if you have big ambitions, you must learn how to operate on a bigger level.

For instance, I teach not only my salespeople about these secrets to success but the clients too. By that I mean that I educate them that my people are an integral part of my team, and that sometimes my clients will be dealing with someone who works with me. But I also develop that trust with the client so that they know I will always be available if they need me. That will always be true—because as you grow, you cannot ignore these basic steps so essential to building trust, so important to your integrity. When you lose trust and integrity, you will lose your business.

The best thing about my recipe is when I was on a flight recently with my family on vacation, we were in midair when I realized that somehow, somewhere, someone is selling a house for our company. It's an incredible feeling.

Now, some of this book is about the path to success for people who want to go into sales or into a career in real estate. But these success principles apply to clients and investors as well. Here's an example of the small steps for one of them.

If you are unfamiliar, in New Zealand, rugby is a passion, and our national treasure is a team called the All Blacks. They have won the international World Rugby Cup three times (the only team to do so). I mentor some of the men on the team.

One of these men on the team was renting a house for $750 a week, and he was earning great money. I said, "Look, what you earn in salary in a year playing rugby, I will make you the same in investments eventually."

When he bought his first house, I said, "I want you to be worth ten million dollars when you finish your career." What? *Yes!* Because most rugby players, most professional sports players, will be poor after their career. This is a phenomenon around the world, no matter whether the sport is American baseball or football or soccer in Europe. For example, within two years of retirement, 78 percent of NFL players are either bankrupt or in financial difficulties. For the NBA, within five years of retirement, 60 percent are broke.[1]

I want to change this. I call it Life after Sports. I give these players the recipe—not to sell real estate (though I would happily train them to do so after retirement) but to invest in steps to build wealth.

After three years, this player couldn't believe it. He was worth $6 million. He called me around the time he got an update from his portfolio of investments.

"Me and my wife, we walked outside with what you sent us, and we keep on walking back and forth on the lawn of our beautiful home, knowing we are invested in other properties, and we can't believe what we achieved in the space of three years following your plan."

The following sales chart illustrates how I achieved this for him and his family.

---

1 Pablo S. Torre, "How (and Why) Athletes Go Broke," March 23, 2009, https://vault.si.com/vault/2009/03/23/how-and-why-athletes-go-broke.

	PRICE PER PROPERTY	RENT PER ANNUM	NEW VALUE
1st Property	$500,000	$31,200	$750,000
2nd Property	$970,000	$57,200	$1,450,000
3rd Property	$550,000	$36,400	$850,000
4th Property	$550,000	$33,800	$850,000
5th Property	$550,000	$33,800	$850,000
6th Property	$720,000	$39,000	$1,100,000
Totals	*$3,840,000*	*$231,400*	*$5,850,000*

As the values of the properties increase naturally over time and with the work you invest in them, if you take that new valuation (in this example, the total of $5,850,000) and subtract your original purchase price ($3,840,000), you'd have a total capital gain of $2,010,000.

Then, using the new valuations total of $5,850,000 and an average capital gains rate of 8 percent per annum, you can calculate that you would gain an additional $468,000 in the next twelve months from those properties.

The following chart illustrates what the capital gains could be after ten years, at a growth rate of 8 percent per annum:

End of 1st Year	$6,318,000
End of 2nd Year	$6,823,440
End of 3rd Year	$7,369,315
End of 4th Year	$7,958,860
End of 5th Year	$8,595,568
End of 6th Year	$9,283,213
End of 7th Year	$10,025,870
End of 8th Year	$10,827,941
End of 9th Year	$11,694,177
End of 10th Year	$12,629,711

As you can see, after ten years, the total value of the assets is over $12,000,000!

Now, we must never limit ourselves. I do want him to go to $10 million, just like I told him. But then when he gets to $10 million, in the long-range plan, eventually in the next ten years, he'll be worth $20 million.

As a sports player, rugby players are such masculine men and they can seemingly run through brick walls. But when it comes to numbers, some are just like little kindergarteners. They need to be taught how to walk, how to run, how to do building blocks. The small steps. But once they learn how to talk my language, they learn the investment aspect of real estate.

Taking small steps also means having patience. I never sell anyone a property on my first meeting. I sell someone a property after the third or the fourth meeting. So, therefore, naturally I assess them, and they go away, think about it, and I assess them again. Most agents will want to sell somebody a house on the spot—because that agent was only interested in themselves. *I'm interested in the people themselves.*

Patience, trust, integrity. Then once you acquire that trust, they can then trust you with their lives. People's homes are usually the biggest investment they will make. It certainly is imbued with emotions.

Integrity means you do not betray that trust—you do not abuse the power you have over someone's savings and money. Many people abuse relationships of trust (false trust and integrity!), meaning they take advantage of people.

I never abuse my position of power. The minute you abuse your position of power, you will never be the same again.

I am a bit like a real estate doctor. Let's say you go to the doctor with a headache or stomachache and you do not feel well. What sorts of questions will the doctor ask?

The doctor will say, "Oh, what did you eat last night? What did you drink?" You tell the doctor everything. You trust them to get to the root of the problem. You trust them to have integrity to not prescribe something that you do not need or that will harm you.

When you come to Don Ha, the Wealth Doctor, I will ask, "Well, what's your income? What does your spouse or partner do? How many kids do you have? What paths to success are you on? Do you own a house? How much savings do you have? Any bad debts? What do you want to be? What kind of lifestyle do you aspire to?"

Very few Realtors take the time to truly exercise compassion and get to know their client. Let's say, the person tells me, "My first priority is to get into my first family home."

As their Wealth Doctor, I probe. "OK, we'll find your first home. Give me a description of the home you want."

I remember one of the All Blacks telling me, "We want a five-bedroom home."

I said, "Why do you want a five bedroom when there's only two of you?"

He told me, "Well, when I play rugby, my family can come and stay with me and watch me play, so I'd like to have a house where my family will stay with me."

Shortly after the call, one night, I was researching the area he desired, even though it is an hour's drive from my office. (Research is another non-negotiable element to success.) I went and looked at all the listings in the community where he wanted to live, and I assessed all the five-bedroom homes. Then I went and saw this one house that in my gut I knew was perfect for him.

Before he even saw it, I said, "Prepare to cry when you see this house." Because I just knew it was the perfect house for him. When he turned up, honest to God, he cried. He bought the house. He didn't even *look* at any other houses. He bought *that* house.

I'm a master matchmaker to hunt for people's needs and wants.

That property was not even on my listing, on top of that. I didn't even get a large commission. In the middle of the night, I was lying on my couch, lights off. I thought about it to myself at that moment. I said, "You must be the craziest person in the world. Nobody else would work so hard to make a sale for so little commission." Especially for a person in my position.

Except nobody else is like me. I know having integrity is essential to every aspect of success. You may succeed without integrity, but that success will not be long-lasting.

Now that same guy has a portfolio of almost $6 million.

Before we leave this chapter, I want to share two other steps you must take.

The first is to learn to listen. *Truly* listen. My talent is being able to shut up and listen to everybody for thirty minutes and then ask one more question and listen for another twenty minutes. I listen a lot before I speak. Listening is an art form. Most salespeople tell clients what good Realtors they are but take no interest in the client's situation, such as job, income, children, what schools their kids go to, and hobbies, and there is no compassion or relationship building to create trust.

Think about social media, which is so confessional. Everybody is always just telling everything about themselves online and not really listening. I have approximately seven thousand contacts in my phone. But I have a habit (a consistent, small step!) of calling ten people before ten in the morning. And it doesn't have to be for business. Most of my calls are to say hello and see how they are and give them market commentaries, or advice, and the business naturally follows from the relationship.

Many people will tell me I need Facebook. I need email. I need this. I need that. Honestly, in business, I don't need any of that. I just go to my contact list, and I see people in real life. I see a minimum of eight to ten people per day face to face. And I've been seeing them like that for my whole career.

The small steps you need to take are to make connections, real connections.

Finally, I want to share about two people in my company. First, let's start with my chief operating officer (COO). In fact, now she's a shareholder, a director in RE/MAX New Zealand, the master franchise. She started with the company about eighteen years ago, and then, she was an administrator only. When she arrived, she naturally started at the bottom rank of the company and dealt with other senior management people, who were her supervisors.

As time passed, eventually, she kept on learning and never complained about long hours or the hard work involved. In fact, she had another job offer from another company, and it was for more money, and I said to her then, "If you'll stay in our company, you will become very successful in the future. And I'll make you a millionaire at it. And that's your choice."

This is truth—I don't make false promises.

She stayed. And then after her first year, she felt pressured by advice from others, and she considered resigning. I said to her, "If you leave now, you will be a quitter—your goals are in sight."

She stayed and kept on going on her plan, listening to my advice, and learning the ropes in all areas of the company. Other people left the company (as people will do), and she kept at her goals, one small step at a time.

Today she's COO of RE/MAX New Zealand, she's a shareholder, and she's a director. And now, believe it or not, the people who tried to persuade her to leave the company are still salespeople.

I obviously recognize her value in what she does. I appreciate her hard work. But I did not make her the COO. Of course, yes, I promoted her. But it was her integrity, her ability to set goals, work hard, and her not losing sight of what she wanted to accomplish that also hugely contributed, as well as seeing how respected she is by her peers.

When I interview people, I look at what they want out of life. Their goals are very important. I like to hear things like, "I want to work in this company because it will offer me the road map to financial freedom to provide for my family. And I always wanted to do this because I am sick of earning average money."

Another young man came to work for me. He said, "Give me anything that you don't want to do or other people don't want to do. I'll take all the leftovers and I'll work my way up."

When I see someone like that, I know they have that fire. This young man came aboard, and he was a bit of a troublemaker and, in fact, had even been in trouble with gangs. But I saw that fire, and I saw his goal setting, and I was willing to take a chance on him.

Today he's married, has two kids, and has his own company employing over a hundred people, and we are still good friends even though we are competitors. So when you help others, you are not only improving their life, but the tentacles of that help fan out and transform other people's lives as well.

Sometimes, with small steps, you may not see your progress. But keep at it, because one day, you will turn around and see that, in fact, you have come so far from where you started.

That is the pathway to exponential success. Transformation and then progress, one step at a time.

PART II
RICHES

CHAPTER 4

RELEASING LIMITATIONS

Limits, like fears, are often just an illusion.

—MICHAEL JORDAN

Most of us carry a secret inside us—that one thing (or possibly many things) that we think holds us back. For some of us, we treat it like a rare orchid. We water it, nurture it. We feed into it, just like we feed orchids plant food.

For example, someone might be insecure because of a stutter (something US President Joe Biden has) or an aspect of their appearance. Someone else might feel insecure because they grew up impoverished. Or because they did not finish college. Someone may feel they are too short; another that they are too tall and tower over people. Another may think they are not smart enough. The reasons for self-doubt and limitation-oriented thinking are as varied as there are people in the world.

But what if we turned that around? What if, for example, we said, "Growing up without advantages taught me the value of 'hustle' and hard work"? Now the negative is a positive. We spin it backward on its axis.

No Excuses Thinking

On paper, if I listed some of the so-called strikes against me, it might look like I should not succeed. Here are ten reasons I should not have been successful. (And I could come up with more!)

- I started in real estate not speaking English well.

- I felt inferior dealing with people who were more successful than me or who appeared to be. I was an Asian man in a field in which most of the successful people were and are Caucasian and spoke fluent English.

- I was not born and brought up in New Zealand.

- I was a refugee.

- I had no local area knowledge and struggled to ready maps.

- I had exactly zero real estate sales experience.

- My family and community of origin did not believe in me or did not think that I would be successful in my new career.

- I am not very academically inclined.

- I had no mentors or role models in my community for what I was trying to do.

But I have never been one to accept limited thinking.

Now, once I sold those eighty-six homes, I suppose I could have thought to myself, *This is a great career. I'm satisfied with my new level of income.*

But the art of exponential success means not being satisfied—it's setting the next goal. And the next. And the one after that. With no limits on your mindset.

Satisfied but Not Satisfied

I decided I wanted to be a millionaire by age thirty. (I accomplished that before I was thirty.) I wanted to get married and have a family. (That too.) But then when you achieve the things you aspire to, what's next?

I have observed that there are three kinds of people in the world:

- The person who is never satisfied. They have no optimism. They see the glass as half-empty. When success comes their way (which won't be often with a defeating attitude), they immediately are waiting for the other shoe to drop. Or they gripe because it's not quite what they want, or it doesn't live up to their expectations.

- The person who is too satisfied. This type of person is so common in my industry that I might call it a phenomenon. I have many Realtors I encounter or who have worked for me—I am even related to some people with this mindset—who are satisfied with their income. They can pay the bills without too much stress and take a nice vacation each year. They drive a decent car. And they stay there. Just coasting. I do think it is terrific to be happy and content with where you are in life, but I think if you are "too satisfied," then you just stagnate.

- The person who is satisfied but not satisfied. This is someone who expresses gratitude for the good things in life. But they want to be continually challenged—they want to climb that next mountain.

Guess which category I fall into?

My Real-Life, No-Limits Story

I am going to tell you the absolutely true story of my no-limits mindset and a little bit of how I built my empire.

Initially, you may recall, in my first year in real estate, I was in the bakery where I was earning around $30,000 a year. In my first year in real estate, I earned $220,000 a year. That's a lot of money. That is money beyond what most people can imagine—that exponential leap is like earning eight years of income in one year. That kind of leap transforms your financial life. It's a whole change in your life and circumstances, a complete shift.

So then from there, I adjusted and expanded my mindset. I lost any sense of limitation or timidity in my dreams. Anything was possible! For my next goal, I wanted to double my income every year. And that next year, I did. I went from $220,000 a year to $440,000. Now that's crazy money. That was money beyond what my family could have ever imagined leaving Vietnam with nothing.

But I knew I could do more. Like this book title, I wanted exponential growth and success.

So now that I knew I could double my income, I was not intimidated by the next leap (you must have brave goals!).

After earning $440,000 a year, I said, "OK, now I want to earn a million in one year."

A friend once joked, "You actually won't have a million, because if you get a divorce, your wife will take half." (My wife has been one of my biggest supporters, but I did think, *OK, just to challenge myself I will aim for $2 million.*)

However, something happened when I got to $500,000. I ran out of time.

By this I mean, I couldn't be in two places at once. I couldn't take two phone calls at once. I could not visit two clients at once. I could not show two properties at a time. Unless I cloned myself, there was a limit, despite my mindset, on what I could accomplish. So, this required growing in a different way.

I had to get a personal assistant (PA). The person I hired was a licensed real estate professional, and I trained her to handle some of the real estate transactional details and sales. Then I added another assistant to handle all the office functions. Now obviously employing people to work for you and with you is a big turning point. I have found it is often one of the biggest stumbling blocks to moving up to the next level of success. People feel they can't hire assistants or employees because they think they will lose control. They think that the PAs are going to take all their customers, and they think they're going to steal their trade secrets. But people afraid of taking this step forget one important thing—the relationship you have with your customers and your vendors. That should be your secret weapon. I have found because I nurture those relationships, those customers will follow me wherever I go.

Adding these assistants took me to $800,000. Obviously, since you know my mindset by this point in the book, I said, "OK, now I want to reach $1.6 million in commissions." But by the time I got to $1.6 million, I realized I was running out of time again. That's when I began coaching and teaching and leading seminars. Instead of talking to people one-on-one (which I still do, of course), I was now talking to thirty, forty, or a hundred or more people at a time.

I just kept expanding my vision. I had my system and my never-wavering principles of trust and respect. With what I learned I was capable of, I thought, *What the heck, I can do this now.* So, I set an ambitious goal to do a million dollars of commission income each month.

Now, when you have very ambitious goals, it is so helpful to have your partner's or family's support. Very big "reach" goals require big efforts. I said to my wife, "This year I want to do a million a month, and I will be working some crazy hours, but it's for our future and our children's. I need your support." And she was (and is) phenomenal—she keeps our household running so well, efficiently and happily. Her support also meant my children's support—because we are all a team. One of the most wonderful aspects of my career has been watching my children absorb some of these very lessons.

> *Without ambition one starts nothing.*
> *Without work one finishes nothing.*
> *The prize will not be sent to you.*
> *You have to win it.*
>
> —RALPH WALDO EMERSON

That year, I must say, I worked eighty to a hundred hours a week. Between my rental income, my commission income, and my capital gains in my properties, I reached that goal.

This should demonstrate that it is completely possible to double your income. It is possible to more than double it. It is possible to work hard and to transcend from one level of wealth creation to another most people only dream about.

Finally, if I bring you, my readers, to now—instead of doing a million a month, I set a new goal that I want to do a million in a week. And I have achieved that too. Not only that, but I am also often making a million dollars in three hours—not a week, just three hours. Through the technological miracles of Zoom.

Limitless Thinking Requires Letting Go of Fear

I see FEAR all around me in others. Many motivational speakers use this acronym: False Evidence Appearing Real.

We can talk ourselves into almost anything. And we can talk ourselves out of almost anything. Think of my list of ten things that "could" have held me back from success. Many of them are rooted in fear. For example, I could have been afraid of selling because (as many in my community told me) I was an Asian man pursuing greatness in real estate in a country I was not born in.

Think of some of the things you may have talked yourself out of. For example, perhaps you work for someone else and earn a salary and now want to take a commission-based position because of the potential great rewards. However, for most people, their thinking goes something like this:

What if I fail?

What if I don't like my new job and I've already left my other job?

What if I'm not good at it?

What if I lose face?

All of those "what ifs" are FEAR. I see over and over again people achieve a certain level of success, and then FEAR comes in, and they scurry backward. They return to "safety." Or they are stuck. Or, they are too afraid of giving up a steady paycheck to reach for the sky's the limit income.

I have people on staff in administrative positions who earn salaries, and I try to tell all of them to expand their knowledge and to study our company and how we do things, encouraging them to pursue the goal of moving into sales. I want each and every person who works for me to have limitless success.

Some do. And they are inevitably successful and see their income shoot up if they work hard and follow my advice. Some do not—they are afraid of taking that step.

Now I am going to help you replace your FEAR with a different kind of FEAR.

Fiercely Embrace Acceptable Risk

If you have $100 in your bank account now and you add on one more zero, it's $1,000. You add one more zero, and it's $10,000. You add one more zero, and it's $100,000. You add on one more zero, and it's a million. It's all about the numbers, and it's all about your mind—how you think. You cannot be intimidated by big dreams and big numbers. When I think about the billionaires whom I meet, guess what? They still have to eat a sandwich at the airport. We're all the same. But it's just how our mind thinks. We get intimidated (which is the bad kind of fear).

These concepts may be challenging your mind, but believe you can do it. Assess the risks. One of the definitions of risk is the possibility that an asset may lose value—a *possibility*. But that also means there is a possibility that it will gain in value. Yes, there will always be some things out of your control. The real estate market, for example, is very cyclical—property values rise for several years, and then there is often a boom—and values soar. After a while. There is a market correction, and the prices reflect that. Then guess what? The cycle starts all over again.

The one risk you can control is your own attitude and work ethic. I will back myself every single time.

Collect your resources and your product. List all of your positive qualities (all the reasons you should back yourself). Tell yourself you will not quit. Devote the proper time to your new career ambitions—if other real estate agents were working forty-five hours a week, work seventy. Make sure you have good people around you and look for mentors. You can do it. Remember, if you are just starting out, the main risk is giving up when you face discouragement. If you stick with it, you will be successful. Go after it fiercely, with all you've got.

Surround Yourself with Limitless People

Speaking of the people around you, I need to share about that too. My family, like many people who have gone through hardship, wanted to work hard and play it safe. When you arrive in a new country with nothing in your pockets, then modest income is a relief. You go from being hungry, perhaps, to knowing you can feed your family and put a roof over your heads. But after the traumas of lean times, very often "safety" is valued most.

I saw it all around me. Does this sound familiar? You believe that a certain income is all you can earn because everyone around you is earning that. Your family is earning that; your parents are earning that; your cousin, your brother, sister, your friends, and your friends' families, all are content with their safe place. You've been programmed to earn that level of money.

Now, if all of a sudden you want to earn $250,000, you will be told it's impossible. You can't do it because literally no one around you has done it. So then you convince your mind to believe that's all you can do.

But when you look outside the bubble you are in, you will see a whole other way of thinking.

First, study limitless people. Now, I did not know people outside my community who could mentor me. When I looked around, I saw people who wanted that safety. So, at first, I did the next best thing in search of others to teach me. I studied the masters. At a young age, I discovered Zig Ziglar. So many people have been inspired by him, and the mindset he gave me was so different from my community's and my family's. For example, he said, "The foundation stones for a balanced success are honesty, character, integrity, faith, love, and loyalty."

Even though his mindset was so far from my own, I knew, deep down, that those same values were part of my core. It's funny;

we sometimes think of ourselves as very different. I know, as an immigrant, it was easy for me to see myself as different—and for others to perhaps judge me by my accent or background. But speakers like Zig reminded me that character, hard work, and positive values could lead anyone to success.

I also realized that to truly succeed in my new chosen profession, I had to educate myself—not just on properties and real estate but on world events; the economy and economic cycles; politics around the globe, art, and culture; and all sorts of topics. Part of it was self-improvement. Part of it was that such self-improvement was important so I could converse with all sorts of people on many subjects as I made my way in the world of business.

I also took it upon myself to study successful people. I looked into their habits, and I looked into their hardships. If you get nothing else from this book, I hope you take with you the idea that even if you have had a difficult start in life, you can overcome anything.

From there, it's all sheer, hard work.

Ideally, too, once you have the belief that you are on a new path to success, then you've got to approach someone who's already successful, who has been there, done that. Seek them out, just as you sought out the masters like Zig Ziglar. A mentor will give you some guidance and reinforce your self-belief. If you have ever watched an experienced free climber choosing a path up a mountain, they are creating a trail for others to follow. When you find a mentor, they will point out the best footholds to reach the top of the mountain.

In addition, once you are on your climb, you need to look around and see who is climbing with you. Ask yourself who are the people you hang out with. For example, if you're going to hang out with people who party all the time and smoke and drink, that is a likely reflection of who you are going to become. If you hang out with people who blow their money frivolously, or who don't want to work too hard, who take the lazy way, then you will be tempted to do the same.

So, you've got to change your surroundings by hanging out with people who believe in you and people with high aspirations.

The Power of Self-Belief

Self-belief is your superpower. Think of Iron Man. His arc reactor powers his artificial heart. Your inner reactor is self-belief and confidence. With each success, you build up that reactor and supercharge it. For example, as you will learn in this book, I have experienced huge setbacks. No successful man or woman has a straight path to massive success. There are too many variables, and any time you aim high, there are risks.

But self-belief will enable you to face downturns, U-turns, and the inevitable hard times. I think of it like this. Suppose you aim high and tell yourself that next year you will make $150,000 in your sales position. And you do it! But then two years go by when you miss the mark. Here is when you use the power of self-belief to remind yourself that persistence and determination got you there once before, and they will get you there again. You've learned you can do it. Think of what a gift that is.

In 1994, I told the boss of the real estate company where I was starting that I wanted to earn $50,000 a year. That was a lie, actually. I wanted to earn much more. I saw the number one earner at his firm made $160,000. I studied her and knew she worked about fifty hours a week. So I said to myself that I would work seventy hours—and that led to $220,000 in a year!

This was so important and valuable. While the money was life-changing for me at the time, what it did for my self-belief was even more incredible. That was when I realized my limitation was being programmed by my surroundings. I "thought" I could work harder than anyone and beat anyone else's earnings. But at that point it was a theory. An idea. After that year, I saw it in action, and it just fueled my arc reactor.

Out-Goal Your Competition

This is what happened to me. I supercharged my arc reactor. I out-goaled the first real estate company where I worked. Then I out-goaled all the mentors I met along the way. So, I have no mentors in that sense. My only mentors today are the successful people whom I read about in books and admire.

Now, I do have advisers. I have a lawyer friend, for example. I've known him for over twenty-five years, and I can bounce ideas off of him. I have also learned from the people I have sold houses to, the people from all different backgrounds. I have learned from their mistakes and their successes. I apply every lesson I learn and observe.

A Real-Life Mentoring Success Story

You can do this. And to prove it to you, I'm going to share a success story—but not mine. Someone I mentored and advised.

I had one client in my first couple of years in real estate. He was working for a fast-food chain, the world's favorite burger franchise at the time, and I sold him his first home for $75,000. I stayed in touch, and I remember meeting his wife and his first daughter, who was born in this very low-cost housing area in South Auckland. Over the next five to seven years, I mentored him as his home's value grew. I sold him his second house, which he bought by being very focused and frugal. And then when I met him again a few months later, he said, "Hey, I've been promoted to general manager now."

As an aside, self-belief isn't about just one area of your life—it's all the areas. Not just real estate, but any career.

I told him to save his money, and I would sell him another home as an investment property. Meanwhile, his self-confidence and self-belief kept growing. He saw himself not only as a general manager, but he saw himself as an investor as well. Next, he was promoted to area manager. I told him we would repeat the same process—and invest in another property. Over seven years, I sold this man seven properties!

Success builds on success. When you are excited and challenged and can see dreams coming true, you tend to work harder. He was very driven, and then the company he worked for offered him an opportunity to buy his own fast-food restaurant. Because of the wealth creation and equity I had been steadily building for him, and my advising, he was able to make the leap to a franchise owner.

As of this writing, he owns three fast-food restaurants and employs over 350 people. And this story is not over! He keeps on building his empire.

I want you to think about that reach. This one person whom you helped now is helping 350 people and their families and their children. That's like a small town being helped by one person's exponential success.

Opportunity Knocks

One last story before we move on to the next chapter.

An immigrant texted me. He had been in New Zealand for well over half his life, and he was quite shy. He had some questions about buying a home that needed a great deal of rehab (he is very handy), and he was seeking my advice. I have a very soft spot for people who are immigrants or who perhaps are just dipping their toe into the investment world.

I'm the sort of person who replies to everybody regardless—again, it is so important to never forget where you came from. I replied to him and said, "Look, I can see you in person to give you some advice."

He was not expecting this. People do not expect the CEO of all of RE/MAX of New Zealand to personally reply to a text asking for advice. And he texted me, "Tell me where, any time, any day." I thought it was a really positive sign that he was so determined to see me. So, then I texted, "Okay come today at noon and I will meet with you for thirty minutes."

He turned up as promised. I gave him half an hour of my time. I advised him what to do. He was not making ends meet, but he had some equity. I said,

"You should be investing some of your money in these properties that are being built and then I would delay selling it for the next eighteen months. And then when their value goes up by a hundred thousand, you will earn a hundred thousand on your $80,000 deposit. And you should buy and sell two or three of these in a year so that way you can make a new salary on top of your existing salary."

I also introduced him to a mortgage broker to help him with his loan approval for these potential purchases.

Then I said, "I've got a seminar tomorrow, why don't you come?" In general, I am always looking for determination in a human being or how determined they are to learn. Sure enough, the next day he came to the seminar.

A millionaire from Australia, a developer, was presenting at our seminar. At the end of the night, the man I'd invited along with me was the last one there, and I told him the presenter and I were going out to dinner and invited him to come along with us—he accepted on the spot. He was still quite shy at dinner, mostly observing.

After dinner, I said, "Tomorrow I have another seminar, but it's a bigger audience. If you're not doing anything, if I were you, I'd turn up." And he said, "OK, I'm turning up."

It was amazing—I saw his shyness falling away a little at a time. Now, his life is transformed—he has been like a sponge soaking up the knowledge of these seminars and the people he is meeting (remember, surround yourself with people going in the same direction as you up the mountain). He's making investments—and setting his sights on bigger goals. He is confident, and his entire bearing has changed.

I encourage people to look for the opportunity, but also don't turn the opportunity down when it's been offered to you. If it knocks, you'd better answer the door.

Recap and Review

OK, this chapter has been about releasing limitations and about the power of self-belief. Let's revisit some of the points that are important to retain:

- *Embrace no excuses thinking.* Other people, your family of origin, or your friends, or even teachers and others may tell you that you do not have the necessary elements to be successful. Don't believe them. Anyone who works hard enough and is driven enough can be successful. Look at all the supposed strikes against me. I never let them stop me.

- *Fiercely Embrace Acceptable Risk:* This should be your new definition of FEAR.

- *Understanding self-belief is your superpower.* Like Tony Stark's arc reactor, self-belief can fuel your ambitions.

- *Surround yourself with limitless people.* Look around you. What are your friends' habits? Do the people around you lift you up and believe in you or put down your dreams?

- *When opportunity knocks, answer the door.* Pursue success—don't allow chances to pass you by.

CHAPTER 5

SETBACKS HAPPEN TO EVERYONE

Only those who dare to fail greatly can ever achieve greatly.

—ROBERT F. KENNEDY

I 've told you some of my story—how I rose above very difficult circumstances to be where I am now. One of the problems of people seeing your success is they no longer see the struggles.

For example, as of this writing, recently, my beloved New Zealand had absolutely unprecedented ecological disasters. First, we had torrential rains, the likes of which the areas near me had never experienced. On the heels of that, Cyclone Gabrielle tore through. For only the third time in the history of New Zealand, a national state of emergency was declared.

I had some leak issues in my home, but I came through OK. However, as a leader, I had to be concerned about my employees, their families and relatives, and all my company's clients—those whose houses were on the market, about to list, about to close, and those families anxiously waiting to move into their new homes. So in addition to my personal pressures, I needed to provide calm and steady leadership and compassion to the many, many people around me.

Some people will think, *Well, how could Don Ha understand my struggles? He lives in a mansion. He owns a successful and prominent real estate company. He owns a number of luxury cars.*

Just remember what I have been telling you this whole book—whether you're a billionaire or the person who takes orders at the coffee shop—we're all people. We all have to eat and sleep and work. We are all equals, but we can study the successes of others and learn to replicate it.

Success is a bit like an iceberg. You see the pinnacle—the shining icy peak above the water. But most of the dangers remain under the water. You only see part of the iceberg, not the worries beneath the surface.

However, in addition to my refugee-to-business-guru transformation, I experienced a dark setback. During the global financial crisis (GFC), most people in real estate took a tremendous hit. I took one worse than most—I discovered that not everyone is as honest as they portray themselves to be. As a consequence, my company entered into receivership.

From Highs to Lows

When I became rookie of the year and number one salesperson at the start of my career, that was a high point in my life. I remember sitting in my seat at the banquet feeling almost numb with pride, joy, and a feeling like I should pinch myself. In a single year, I had transformed my financial life. I had also transformed how I saw myself—I now knew, beyond a shadow of any doubt, that I had no limits to success. I was later number one in another company and the international number two of the year. For a person without a degree, who had learned English only in his teens, with a background of a refugee camp, that was beyond what I could ever imagine.

I was at the height of my game and then along came the GFC and the lowest point of my life. I went into receivership and lost everything. I felt worse than when I came here as a twelve-year-old refugee, because my control was taken away from me.

In a receivership, the bank takes over your company—immediately. They chop it into pieces, selling off furniture and equipment, and then try to find a buyer for what's left.

It wasn't like your typical agent or businessperson going into receivership—I was perhaps the biggest name in real estate in New Zealand going through this. Depending on which publication was being read at the time, when the receivers moved in, they took with them the tattered dreams of a refugee who thought he'd made it only to have the rug pulled out from under his feet a few yards from the mountaintop. But those dancing on my grave by way of the comment boards knew nothing of the resolve lingering inside me.

There is an eighteenth-century word the English language has borrowed from Germany: *schadenfreude*. It means delighting in someone else's misfortunes. We see this in celebrity culture, where people breathlessly read online about this movie or athletic star getting into trouble or losing their fortune. Because these stars are wealthy and famous, people are often a little jealous of them—so that when something goes very awry in their lives, there is a secret guilty pleasure in watching them fall from grace.

Because of the way in which I had taken the real estate world by storm and my unprecedented success, there were those just lying in wait like wolves, waiting for me to behave like an injured lamb.

That was not to be the case.

scha·den·freu·de

/'SHädən͵froidə/

Pleasure derived from another person's misfortunes.

The Global Financial Crisis

Real estate is cyclical. You can watch prices for homes shoot skyward, and then it reaches, to borrow a phrase from physics, *critical mass*. We call it a "market correction." Home prices are too high, and there is a little pullback. This means prices fall between 10 and 20 percent. Real estate settles down, and then economic or other circumstances will drive the prices up again. For example, during the COVID-19 pandemic, prices were driven higher.

During 2008–2009, for a total of about nineteen months, however, an unprecedented "perfect storm" hit the world—the GFC. There were numerous causes of this storm, which included the following:

- *Subprime mortgages.* This is when mortgage loan requirements are loosened and people are at higher risk of being unable to pay their mortgage (e.g., with higher levels of debt or not a lot of savings). Foreclosures reached a high during the crisis, hitting the real estate market heavily.

- *Wall Street shenanigans.* On Wall Street, investors were buying lenders' packaged subprime loans (and using other elaborate schemes to make riskier investments). There were numerous questionable practices.

- *Lax regulation.* As all of this was going on, at least in the United States and elsewhere, regulators were asleep at the wheel. As is often the case, when things are going great, it's easy to look the other way. It's like a huge party thrown by a college kid. It's all great until someone gets a little too rowdy and the cops have to come.

- *The 2008 stock market crash.* The subprime mortgage loans were like a virus, and the virus spread through the world, eventually contributing to a mighty crash.

The effects were global. This perfect storm didn't just hit New Zealand, or Europe, or Hong Kong, or China. It hit everyone. In a globalized society, investors have their assets worldwide.

The real estate market in New Zealand wasn't immune from this. There was no GFC vaccine. And I was not immune either.

How My Nightmare Unfolded

I remember the night like it was yesterday. On March 16, 2011, on the tails of the recession, I was set to be named the number one real estate office in New Zealand for the real estate franchise I owned.

I was under stress—the real estate market had taken a huge hit. I had just that day written numerous big checks for overdue bills to suppliers. Next, I took several more meetings with major developers who also needed to sell their properties to keep their company afloat.

If you are too young to fully remember the crisis, it was a painful time. While they call it the GFC (as opposed to the Great Depression of the early twentieth century), it was horrible and a very deep recession. I remember seeing people lined around the block applying for a single job. Nightly news programs, all over the world, showed tearful families facing bank foreclosure on their homes.

As an aside, a home is not a house. If you are the right kind of real estate person, you are very aware of this. A house is a structure. A home is a warm place associated with all the feelings you have related to safety, love, and comfort. As a refugee, I know that better than anyone.

I had spent a few sleepless nights because of the crisis, but when you have been a refugee, you know you have been through worse, so I would look for a practical plan rather than just ruminate on worries and fears.

Upbeat, I arrived at the real estate awards ceremony at the plush Sky City Casino in great spirits. While the dramas with the financial crisis were still in front of mind, they were eased by the fact that I would be celebrating the success of my office. Being named the number one franchise was just another award or confirmation that real estate was in my blood.

The master of ceremonies announced my franchise's sales—in the hundreds of millions of properties. Suddenly, the spotlight was on me, and I made my way to the podium, snaking through the tables. At the time, in February 2011, Canterbury in New Zealand had experienced a terrible earthquake. The 6.3 magnitude earthquake followed a previous earthquake of 7.1 the previous year. It killed 185 people and affected the area of Christchurch terribly. As I took my place at the podium to say a few words, I announced a substantial donation toward the Canterbury earthquake fund. Then I gave what those in the audience told me was an inspiring speech about how honored I was to lead the number one office in New Zealand. But I also promised them I would be back the following year accepting the same award (remember, it is important to appreciate your blessings—but always be setting your sights on the next mountain to climb).

The night was a blur of congratulations, people wanting to shake my hand, and seeing my colleagues from my office so proud. But life can sometimes change in an instant.

About twelve hours later, at 10:30 in the morning on March 17, 2011, I was about to take my wife and son shopping and out for lunch at the mall across from my office. I had no idea what was about to happen. When I went outside, I saw three people who had been appointed by my bank, and they asked to see me.

I smiled and said, "I'm sorry, I can't. I'm taking my son to lunch."

They were quite stone-faced. One said, firmly, "We have to meet with you."

Since I was still unsure what this all meant, I said, "OK, but not now. I'm going to lunch." Even though I work many hours, when I am with my family, I try to be very present.

They were fairly insistent that they needed a meeting with me—*now*.

Once again, I declined. I figured I would have lunch with my son and my wife and then phone them when I was back in the office.

However, the tone of the conversation became even more dramatic and serious. "OK, well, if you won't meet with us, then we will have to tell you now. Your bank has appointed us to put your company into receivership."

There are moments that are frozen in your mind like a fly in amber. I was holding my son. My wife was there. I was stunned. Eventually, I handed my son to my wife and told her to take him home. I regret that. I should have said, "The hell with you! I'm going to lunch." There was nothing I could do. Once the decision had been made to put me into receivership, there wasn't anything I could do in that instant. I should never have let my wife and son leave.

These three bank representatives handed me some documents to sign. I refused. Then I did what anyone in that situation should do: I called my lawyer.

I went back inside to my office. I took a moment to calm the thoughts swirling around in my head. The GFC had been a global disaster, but I had not an ounce of worry that the cycle would deliver us to saner financial times. I could not understand the bank not working with me.

I believe in transparency, so I called my key staff in. Within minutes of me telling them what was happening, they were offering me money.

"How much do you need, Don?"

I was deeply touched. I knew I prided myself on the atmosphere of our office, the caring and compassion. I don't tolerate cutthroat techniques and backstabbing. And here, my trust in them was being rewarded.

However, I explained the company accounts were frozen. All the commissions that were owed to them were frozen. The company car, the company credit cards—gone. One of my employees went and got me $15,000 cash and gave it to me. He didn't want to put anything into the bank account in case the receivers got hold of it.

Another one of my loyal employees handed me $9,000. At the time, he did not have much surplus money, but he did that for me. I didn't take it from him. I knew he had a wife and three kids, and being without $9,000 could have impacted them, so I refused. Another agent told me he came to my company with nothing and that I had built up his wealth, so he wanted to give me his car to use. I didn't need his car or the money, but those sorts of gestures made me quite emotional.

The day was dizzying. The three men appointed to put my company into receivership had all my assets frozen within the hour. I knew that though I was reeling, I would be OK. I have always had that confidence. However, my staff had to be very worried—after all, we were together trying to navigate the worst financial crisis in nearly a century. I needed to offer leadership, so I assured them everything would be OK in the end. I guaranteed all of my staff that everything I owed them would be paid back in full. I told them that even if I had to pay their commissions, my family would support me.

Next, I told them they had the option to go and work for another one of the real estate companies around the corner from our office. How could I hold it against them if they did? But I told them,

"Do you just want to be employees, or do you want to rebuild this company? Do you want to approach this rebuilding as equals?

You guys are a part of this company. You can go and be dictated to by a boss, or you can stay, rebuild this company, and we can grow together. What do you want?"

They wanted to remain with me. They wanted Don Ha. They knew there was no other boss like me in this business. I brought some pizza and drinks, and we had a little party. My favorite song we listened to was "Not Afraid" by Eminem. We toasted our next adventure.

> *When something bad happens, you have three choices.*
> *You can either let it define you, let it destroy you,*
> *or you can let it strengthen you.*

— THEODOR SEUSS GEISEL ("DR. SEUSS")

Unbeknownst to me, some of my agents had already been contacted by one of my competitors. My understanding is that he told them that I was broke and that I had no future in real estate anymore. He lured them with a job opportunity with up-front cash and a higher commission incentive. He also told them that my word was worth nothing and reminded them that the agency that oversaw my franchise had taken all my listings (about three hundred at the time). I had nothing, he said.

I lost four staff on March 17.

One of the young agents who left I had employed since he was twenty-two. He'd had a few bad life experiences—he'd been caught up with a gang. I brought him aboard because I think everyone deserves a second chance (something I will talk about more in the next chapter). This young man had become one of my best agents.

When I'd taken him to Los Angeles earlier in the year, we were about to sit down to lunch with some of the wealthiest people in real estate in California when I saw him leaving. I asked him where he was going, and he said he was off to have lunch at a fast-food restaurant. So, I made my excuses, left the high rollers at the lunch table, and went with him. It was an easy decision. I didn't want my mate going off to this fast-food restaurant on his own. On the airplane, I flew economy class so that I could sit with him and the others. And now, he was one of the guys leaving. It didn't hurt too much, because I was pragmatic—I figured he had contributed quite a lot to the company while he was with me. But many of the other staff were hurt by his decision.

Another one who left was a young guy whom I had lent a lot of money to over the years to help him with his debts. I'd given him money to go back to his country of birth to visit his family. And then he left me too. And another guy, I used to pay his rent. I'd given him money to send to his mother. He hadn't made any of that money back through his contribution to the company, but he left too. Even my protégé said nothing in response to gossip in the halls. He didn't try to talk any of them into staying. He just kept quiet. Then he asked for a meeting. I knew at that moment he was like the others—two-faced.

Those last three agents hurt me. I'd invested a lot into them. Not just money but time and wisdom, advice, and guidance. I thought they were my right-hand men. Like plenty of people in the corporate world, I thought I had key people who I figured would be with me "no matter what." But this is a cautionary tale for anyone in the corporate world who thinks like that. If I'd walked into our office with those three guys and had been confronted with three hostage takers, the scenario that would have played out would have been this: I would have told my right-hand man to take down the first hostage taker in front of him and my left-hand man to take the second guy. The third man I would have told to help out the hostages while I take the guy in the middle.

Well, in reality, in that story, I would have been killed, because before the confrontation would have started, my guys would have run out of the building! I would have been dead. These were people I had invited to my house, who had met my kids and my wife—some of them even knew about the safe in my house. These are the people whom I gave money to so that they could take it home to their countries of origin to help their families. And they still abandoned the ship.

Once I got back on my feet, they wanted to return.

Normally I would be open to bringing them back, welcoming them back to the nest. But no. Not this time. They kicked me when they thought I was down. They took a pound of flesh out of me and the remaining staff when they walked out on us. I won't ever forget and I am still trying to forgive.

Yes, my competitor could say I had nothing. But he was wrong. I had Don Ha. I had the wealth of my experiences. I had all the knowledge I had gained from eating, sleeping, and breathing real estate for decades. That was not going to go away! They might have been able to take out the office furniture, and they could even put a padlock on the door if they wanted. But they could never take my work ethic or my smarts and know-how from me. Remember this any time you feel kicked when you are down!

In any case, despite the turmoil around me, I was remarkably calm. And because I was calm, I was focused. I am not afraid of a new challenge.

I am not sure why, but in the midst of all this, I suddenly remembered a movie I saw years before. *Heat* pits Robert De Niro's character, career thief Neil McCauley, against Lieutenant Vincent Hanna—the Los Angeles Police Department (LAPD) detective played by Al Pacino. During one scene, McCauley—who seemingly had it all—had the chance to get out of the life he was living. But he couldn't. His life—what he was doing—was in his blood. So, there I was, dealing with the receivers coming in, and I was randomly thinking about De

Niro and Pacino. I realized that real estate was in my blood. This was a blessing, because my mindset was straight away all about finding solutions. I wasn't going to walk away. That idea was utterly laughable. I knew I could buy the company back.

Thus, my mindset wasn't like *what's my wife going to think?* Or, *what's my father going to think?* Or, *what damage will this do to my reputation if this goes public?* If you let yourself go there, then you will be lost down a very dark rabbit hole. I knew I could still control my life, and that made me feel twenty times stronger. On a daily basis, every time I woke up over the next few days, there was a giant in me. I knew I would survive. It was almost like I was in a cartoon. It didn't matter how many cartoon anvils dropped on my head, or how many times Wile E. Coyote tried to destroy me, the clever roadrunner. It didn't matter what people did to try to kill me; I kept getting back up, ready to take another punch if it meant I was going to end up exactly where I needed to end up.

While still fiercely focused, by the time I got home on that first night dealing with this new world, there was anger, and it lasted for a while. That is OK! Anger can be a healthy fuel—what is not healthy is ruminating about it over and over. Anger can be a motivator. Bitterness is a killer.

My first thoughts were, *How could the bank put me into receivership?* They hadn't given me any warning. They should have threatened receivership, and if I didn't pay up, then do what they needed to do. But they never even gave me that chance. They just turned up. In the receivership, it transpired that I had signed a General Security Agreement with them five years prior. I wasn't even aware of that. It meant that I had given them my real estate company as security. Because my company had defaulted on the loan, they put this company in receivership to get their money back. I could have sold the properties held by the company to pay their loan back—there was no need for this sort of nuclear option.

The lesson here is to never give your company away. Always, before you sign a document, make sure you ask about what happens in the worst-case scenario. In the good times, you often sign documents happily. Make sure to have a good legal team and get a second independent legal opinion.

Like many successful developers and agents, I had lawyers and accountants. When times were amazing, and house prices were rapidly shooting up by the month, the banks had even pursued me about borrowing from them. Each meeting I had with them seemed to result in them offering me more money.

However, through some poor advising, I ended up in a difficult spot. This is why I am so devoted to being a mentor today. I had no one with my kind of success in my community to advise me on some of the bigger issues of exponential growth (which is another reason I wrote this book—to offer the insights to others). Someone once told me that if you go to Harvard or Oxford, you are surrounded with "old money" and "legacy" students, whose families and the circles they travel in have a wealth of experiences in investment capital or how to structure a corporation with many divisions. My experiences selling dented tins of baked beans and spaghetti did not prepare me, and without the right advice, it turned out that my financial position was vulnerable. I will obviously never let that happen again.

Anger Can Be a Motivator— Bitterness Is a Killer

By March 19, a Saturday, the media was reporting the story. The headline was "Real Estate King in Financial Trouble."

By noon I had responded to the media in a press release.

Essentially, I said that this was not the end and that my staff were standing by me (except for those four, the rest were determined to help in any way they could). I thanked customers for the calls of support I had received (which were many). The release went on to say:

> Without going into too many details it came to my attention recently that some of the management controls and reporting systems employed by Don Ha Real Estate Ltd weren't what they should have been. I am confident that the bank which put me into receivership doesn't have a true understanding of my position. I wish they had communicated with me more before taking their action because this could have been avoided. Regardless, I am confident that within time this situation will be cleared up. We will continue to work with the receivers and work towards the best outcome for the business. The main message today is that there is no reason for anyone connected with any of my businesses to be worried. It is very much a case of "business as usual." Agents are still being paid, and vendors will continue to list properties.
>
> This whole episode will be a great learning for everyone on my management team. I am extremely positive about the future of Don Ha Real Estate Ltd and anyone who knows me will feel the same.

The media story—which carried the press release—led to much venting from many outsiders looking in. Much of the public response was positive. They ranged from message board postings like "Keep your head up, bro," to this from someone signed ex-employee:

"Don, you are, still are, and always will be the greatest! You taught us so much ... gave selflessly to so many ... inspired us to dare to be different and aim for the stars! All the best Don to you and your family—loved being part of the Ha Team—I know you'll be back!"

Others wondered if this is all a part of my own grand plan (something I chuckled at): "Knowing Don, he will be back in no time. He has solutions for everything. Just wait and see."

But there were plenty of negative posts too. All, of course, under the banner of "Anonymous." Some at least had some humor. "I hope Don hasn't forgotten how to collect watercress," wrote one character. Another simply offered this: "Don Ha ha ha ha." But there was an undercurrent of hate too. Some attacked my character (also laughable if it wasn't so ugly to read).

I will never succumb to that hate. We see it in politics, in some business competition. It's something we see all around us online, sadly. I have remained steadfast in my belief that we need to mentor others, lift others up, offer second chances, and be a mentor. I not only have mentored employees, but I consider getting families into their first home a lifting up. I will advise *any* of my clients on how to save, how to make the money work, and how to budget. Earlier I wrote that a true home is not just a house. I love making the dream of home ownership a reality for people. That's what gets me excited to this day.

So, I remained determined to "go high" when they "went low." Some people in the industry—people who claimed to be my friends— even had the nerve to contact my lawyer to find out how they could acquire some of my assets. And these people—even when they were going behind my back—were being "supportive" by sending me text messages or emails. I can confirm that in this business, sometimes your best mates are your worst enemies.

The experience was a real wake-up call, because the people doing it were people I had seen as peers—people I had taken to lunch on plenty of occasions to share management experiences with.

Some were close mates, or so I thought. They pretended to be nice in front of me, and then, behind my back, they were trying to find out how much they would have to spend to rip my company out from under my feet. It was no different from the Roman days. It was warfare—the only difference was my enemies wore business suits and drove Mercedes or Porsches.

The publicity around the receivership led to dozens of calls from friends and family checking in to see that I was OK. I was. The first thing I did was to make sure that I was still in control. When you are in the moment, you have to make a decision. *Can I deal with this?* Of course, I could! I couldn't control what was being written in the newspapers, but I could control my own destiny. It is in the moment when someone thinks *I can't deal with this* that some celebrities or well-known people in business who face destruction or ruined reputations and slander decide to check out. They commit suicide. Or they turn to alcohol and drugs. Both are reckless, tragic paths. I don't drink, and I don't take drugs. I did not appreciate the falsehoods that proliferated at this point. However, the public doesn't control me. They don't pay my bills.

I had learned to be comfortable with myself. I will be honest, at one point in my life when real estate was high-flying, my real estate firm took on the role of a sponsor for a prominent race event during the annual Auckland Cup horse race held at the esteemed Ellerslie Racecourse. I also bought (at that time) the most expensive racehorse in New Zealand for $2 million with the idea of putting him out to stud and create a legacy in the racing world. It was great public relations. But after a time, I very thankfully realized that recognition by the public and others is not ultimately satisfying—not like having a family or being comfortable in your own skin. I watched many an acquaintance spend their fortunes on things that did not make them content. So, while the circumstances were challenging, I did not let them destroy me.

My profile had remained high in the real estate world since my first big successes, however. This was a good thing—if you see my smiling face peering out from a billboard and you have name recognition, then the publicity is positive. Even buying the racehorse was a positive, because me standing next to the horse was plastered on every newspaper and magazine cover globally. But publicity can be a double-edged sword.

Having a high profile can be bad if, for example, you are doing the wrong things. If you're a public figure and you are caught up in disorderly behavior, you only have yourself to blame. If you rip people off, you deserve to be exposed. When you become well known, you have to accept that 10 percent of the press coverage is going to be negative. That's a fact. And when that negative press comes, you mentally have to program yourself to remember that 90 percent of the coverage is good. You can put up with the negative 10 percent even then, though it's not right.

In every business, there will always be unhappy customers. That's a reality because you cannot guarantee 100 percent happy customer outcomes. There'll be unpaid bills. Staff disputes. Contract disputes. And just because it gets into the paper doesn't mean that you are a bad person. The reporter writing the story doesn't know the ins and outs of your business. You have to ignore the noise (both good and bad).

I'm not saying it's easy. There is no rule book when it comes to dealing with bad press, and no one is successful without making mistakes. If I make a mistake, I can pass the learnings on to my staff or my academy students. Mistakes can be blessings. They make you stronger.

So, my only real concern was my family and staff—they were far more important than some guy down the road reading the newspaper making a judgment on me and what I stand for after scanning one story on a Saturday morning. My wife struggled with it. She would go to school with the kids, and she felt like everyone was staring and gossiping about her. I don't know if they were or not, but it didn't matter. Whether they were staring and gossiping or not, she felt like they were, so for her, it was real.

"That's because you let them think that," I told her. She could not easily handle the pressure. Me? I walked everywhere with my head held high. But at first I didn't want to go out in public. I hid for a couple of weeks. But I came to realize that the perceptions of people I didn't know didn't bother me. So, when I dropped the children off at school, it would be like any other day. I'd go to the shops and restaurants I normally would go to. Some people would stare and whisper, but who cared? They didn't know what I knew. And I knew I would emerge from this stronger than ever.

However, the situation wasn't helped when, within a week, the master franchise (the larger agency of which my franchise was a part of) terminated their support. At first they had said (at least publicly) that they would stand by my side through the receivership process. But then they bowed out completely, stating, "We are now of the opinion that our involvement would not be advisable. We have full confidence that the receiver can achieve the best possible result for all parties, and we support their appointment."

I was truly on my own to figure out a way to recover. But never count me out!

Recap and Review

- Success is like an iceberg. It includes what you can see and what's below the surface. But remember, we are all people.

- Success is not guaranteed. You can indeed go from the highs to the lows quickly—you must be mentally prepared. Don't let the highs of success feed your ego. Don't let the lows of setbacks destroy you.

- Always be aware of everything you sign. And for that matter, make sure you can trust your lawyers and accountants. Get a second independent legal opinion.

- Loyalty is the result of how you treat people. You cannot buy true loyalty.

- No one can ever take away your wisdom and experience. Yes, things happen and you can be attacked in business and lose money. But you are your most valuable asset.

CHAPTER 6

TIME TO REBUILD

Don't be afraid to start over.
It's a new chance to rebuild what you want.

—JIM ROHN

ometimes when you have nothing left to lose, it can be freeing. It was time for me to enter the rebuilding phase.

My first priority in those early days after the receivership occurred was to look after my staff. Looking at the faces of my best people in the local coffee shop I'd taken them to when I was told that my master franchise had taken all of our listings, it was like seeing something worse than a family death in their eyes. They were defeated. They were frightened. They were numb. That truly pained me.

When I went home that day, I jumped in the freezing cold swimming pool, and I kept my head under the water for two minutes. I needed to cool down and clear my mind. I needed to have a plan.

Over the next days, I approached two other major real estate firms about the possibility of gaining a franchise. But they were afraid of bad publicity and were uncomfortable moving forward. My name was suddenly tainted.

My team and I were put in a corner, our hands chopped off. When you are put into receivership, your licenses are revoked, so you don't have anything. You have no business cards, no listings, no computer system—it's all locked away from you. You have nothing. It was like becoming a refugee again. It still made no sense to me that the bank would prefer this than my restructuring and continuing to bring in income.

By this time, I had met with my extended family. I decided I would buy back my own company within three weeks of the day the bank showed up to take it. I was unafraid to announce that. I was going to accomplish this. I had made my family members—siblings, parents, cousins—wealthy far beyond their dreams when we were all in a refugee camp. They knew it was time to help me by loaning me the capital to purchase the business back.

The decision was made to "move" my staff to another agency (one of our main competitors in my area). Then the games started with the receivers. I offered the man who'd taken charge of the receivership process $100,000 to buy the company—minus the rental division.

The receiver said it was worth $300,000. But I told him it was worth nothing but the furniture without the people. If they were going to play hardball with me, I would do the same. I told him that if he didn't take the offer by 3:30 that afternoon, my staff would go and join the competitor. He asked me if he could hold me to that. So, at 3:30 p.m., I had a meeting with my staff and told them to go. I couldn't abandon the ship. I told them I would stay and work with the receivers. And so they went to our rival.

The receivers, all of a sudden, knew that I was serious. They also knew they now had nothing to sell! The people—handpicked and trained by me—were gone. My next offer was $80,000 to buy back the company. The man in charge told me to come up with a little bit more. So now I offered $82,000 (had it been prior to 3:30, it would have been so much more). He came back to me in the afternoon and told me that my bank didn't want to work with me anymore, and they didn't want to support me opening another office.

Fine. Two can play at that game. I told him that my brother would buy the company. He offered them $60,000! (Which I found funny—the offers kept going down.) The receiver stormed off, telling me that he would auction the business off. Ah, yes, cut off your nose to spite your face.

I understood that about seven other people or entities were looking at buying the company. An owner of one of the competing brands came to look at the furniture and equipment at my office. He went to the handful of remaining staff who remained loyal to me and started offering them jobs. He let slip that he heard that someone had offered $500,000 to buy the business with the property management division. That was interesting, because after the "fun" of the previous offers, I had actually offered $500,000 as well! I knew that I was in the hunt to get it back. I kept a straight face. It was one of the best acting jobs of my life.

But, hey, it's easy to act when you're desperate. I knew that if I didn't buy my business back by the next Sunday, my reputation was gone. I had to make this deal happen. So, I made the decision to buy my reputation back. We ended up paying $1,350,000 for it. I paid $100,000 up front and agreed to pay the total on April 17. The receiver came back and said the deal could go through but only if I paid a $400,000 deposit. There was a bit of a standoff. I wanted him to agree to sign the deal before I gave him the money, and naturally, he wanted the money before signing. In the end he got his way—well, almost. He wanted a condition that I couldn't talk about the settlement in the press, among other things. I knew then that the power had shifted back to me. I demanded immediate access to my building. I wanted my listings back, and I wanted them to assist me getting my license back. Then the deal was signed.

Two weeks later, I had my license back.

Two weeks after that, my key staff were back together.

The Sweetest Lemonade

We've all heard the expression, "When life hands you lemons, make lemonade." Well, this lemonade I created was particularly sweet.

As I saw how my master franchise and others treated me, I was now certain I needed to be completely on my own. By this point, I was like the caged bear—sick of being poked and prodded by people on the outside. Sick of people passing judgment on me. Tired of the many people in my business life who had been revealed as having two faces. I am very happy with just one face, thank you. I know who I am when I look in the mirror.

With the wisdom of distance from the events that happened, I realized I had greatly outgrown the agency I had been with. I was consistently number one—in New Zealand! Yet I had been tethered to them. I made great money—for me, for my people, and for the agency. I likely would have stayed for many years out of loyalty and perhaps even comfort.

But now I was free to create my company completely my way.

For the staff who remained, I had a deep appreciation for them, and it went both ways. When my staff went to another agency for two months, it reconfirmed that they had more freedom working for me. That's why we became number one in the first place—we do great business. I don't put restrictions on my staff. I encourage them to come up with their own ideas. I support them. I have relationships with them. I know what's going on in their lives. So, they want to come and work. They want to put in the extra hour at the end of the day to make the sale. That's why when I was back in business, all of my staff whom I truly wanted back left the agency they were working at and came to work for me once again.

The receivership had given me the best opportunity in some ways because it weaned out all the cowboys. And now we were in the ideal position to go forward.

Immediately after I bought back the company, I named it Don Ha Real Estate. Some worried that my name was now mud. I was furious. I worked seventeen years to build my name. I was using it!

My name was already on the building. As we discussed in the last chapter, self-belief is so important. If you don't have self-belief in your own brand or your own ability, how is anyone else going to believe in you? Within one week of becoming Don Ha Real Estate—because I had built up so much goodwill and loyalty in the community I had worked in for so long—I was able to list more than $100 million worth of properties for sale. I'd done a deal with the country's largest building company for another 125 new houses.

I worked harder than I ever had (which is saying a lot since hard work is in my veins). I was always the first one there in the morning and the last to leave, but I found even more time and energy because I wanted Don Ha Real Estate to be three times bigger than the previous company I used to run. I'd always had lots of contact with the customers—now I had more than ever before. I walked the street more. I talked to people. You don't become the prime minister by staying in the office. You have to campaign. That's what I was doing every day. I was campaigning for Don Ha.

I was reinvigorated.

Interestingly, too, if anything the publicity around the receivership had helped. I know that sounds crazy, but bear with me, because it's an important lesson. Many of the customers knew what I had been through, and they saw that I wasn't embarrassed about being in receivership, so they were more open about their own financial situations, and they were more vulnerable. Instead of hiding something, they were now more inclined to share it with me. In a strange way, it was a great icebreaker. I know the opposition tried to use the receivership against me—even to this day. But they don't understand the relationship that I have with the people of Auckland. And overwhelmingly, all the major developers wanted me involved in their projects. The Singaporean developer put me in charge of their development of 162 houses. That's a real vote of confidence. The bank and the press didn't destroy the Don Ha brand. The Don Ha brand was stronger than ever.

Truthfully, I was stronger than ever. I didn't realize I was this strong; I didn't realize that I was this good—to pull off buying back my own company in three weeks, to have the trust of so many people. Prior to the receivership, people thought I was good. Well, now, you can multiply that twenty times. My own father—and he's a very strong man—told me he thought he wasn't as mentally strong as me.

"Anyone else would have given up by now"—that's what he told me when I was going through the receivership.

Before this, on the outside looking in on this, I would have wondered, *How much can one man take?* Well, I have learned that I can handle anything anyone wants to throw at me.

That is power.

My Anchors

This chapter is about overcoming tough times. If you went through tough times, where would you turn? That sacred inner circle includes your anchors. They keep you moored during the rough seas.

Throughout the receivership process, I turned to my six anchors to help me—my wife, my father, my right-hand person, my confidant, my accountant, and my attorney. They were my "go-to" crew.

My wife, Mohini, is a wonderful anchor for me. To have her support, as well as knowing that she takes care of the children and runs the household. She has been a great blessing to me from the earliest days of our relationship and the building of our future. During the receivership of the company, we lost everything, including luxury cars and the mansion we lived in. The most important thing is that I did not lose my wife's trust, loyalty, and belief in me. Throughout our journey, she stood by me.

And my father—he has always been there for me when I needed him most. Whether it is financial assistance or crucial business decisions, he has given me the greatest self-confidence to help me succeed. His values of trust, loyalty, respect, and hard work have now become the values of the company.

When my real estate career was in its darkest hours, my family stood by me, as did my staff, who all provided me with loyalty and moral support. One person gave everything to me by working behind the scenes with suppliers' graphic designers to rebrand and relaunch my company. As my right-hand person, Mala Maharaj has been with the company for almost two decades. Her trust, loyalty, and hard work, her values, and her respect for who I am have helped me through some of the most difficult and challenging times of my life. Her unconditional support and relentless effort have contributed greatly to the success of the business today, and she has treated the company as if it were her own. Many of her colleagues have chosen to invest in real estate for retirement, but Mala has chosen to invest her time and career in the company.

For her loyalty and dedication over almost two decades, I have rewarded her as a shareholder of both RE/MAX New Zealand and RE/MAX Fiji. Currently serving as the chief operating officer (COO), she is now also a director shareholder in addition to acting as COO.

My friend, Ash Patel, is a former top lawyer and a client of mine whom I met in 1994. He's a very high-powered, intelligent, and knowledgeable guy, so when I have any problems, he's one of the first people I want to see, because he can communicate with me. Many people can't relate to me because when I have questions, they are too big, too complicated. But Ash is able to advise me on a number of issues. He is a real confidant, because I can ring him at any hour of the day or night and know that he will have time to meet with me and walk me through whatever it is that I need to be walked through. There is no monetary value in friends—they are priceless.

I have always had a very close relationship with my accountant, Jatin Patel, more like a brother. We have unconditional trust in all our business dealings; whether it is a small transaction or a larger transaction, it does not matter. As well as serving as an adviser to my financial well-being, Jatin has served as an adviser to all my other entities and key employees. As well as creating a vast number of business opportunities for the company, Jatin also provided the best tax solutions.

In restructuring my company, Brett Abraham, my lawyer, has been a crucial facilitator and also a key adviser to the company and senior management staff. Brett was acting on my behalf when dealing with the banks and creditors during the time of my receivership. Brett is the man of experience, a very resourceful, reliable individual who knows and understands the legal system.

Both Brett and Jatin have played a critical role in the restructuring of my company and other entities, and I have known them for over twenty years.

My Lessons

I learned so much from the pain of receivership and the hard work of rebuilding. My focus was now on a thousand-day focus on rebuilding my company and my wealth. I worked harder than when I was a rookie, cutting out all distractions and habits. I didn't smoke or drink, so that part was easy.

For starters, I haven't got time to waste. I am sharper now. I can smell a rat. And rather than put up with an hour-long meeting that is going nowhere, I'll just end the meeting. I am stronger in that way.

Going through the process wasn't easy. It wasn't a walk in the park. I didn't sleep for three weeks straight. One great thing I learned out of this was that every time I was in bed trying to sleep and had a million thoughts rushing through my head, I realized that when you are in the midst of crisis, you must write things down. That helps you come up with the solutions you need.

I also realized that you must never turn down an appointment. In the past, I despised organizing a meeting three or four days ahead of time. It meant that if I woke up that morning and wanted to go have a round of golf with my friends, I couldn't. I wanted to play. But now I want my appointment diary booked up full. Every appointment represents people I can help find and buy their dream home. Appointments are also dollar signs. I see as many people as I can these days because every meeting is potentially more money in the bank—and more people who are satisfied and trust me and my agents because we did right by them.

Another change has been the tightening of my criteria for handing out charity. I have always been something of a philanthropist. I have donated a fair share of my life's income to various charities. These days I prefer to do my charity work in private. You don't give to charity for public relations. Local school and community groups are the main benefactors of my charity. I figure I should support the community that I live in.

In short, I have great clarity.

There is an old Chinese proverb: "He who seeks revenge should remember to dig two graves." I was very angry about the receivership, but I am not angry at one person. Sure, it felt personal, but it's business against business. That's my best revenge. The numbers. The reputation. The reach of my company.

My motivation now is that, by the time I leave this world, I want the Don Ha brand to be my legacy. I want the next generation of people in my family and company to continue to provide teachings and knowledge that I have shared with them.

Through all of the things associated with the receivership, I have come out of it a happier person, because I've now found the real Don Ha. Ultimately, with some of the negative experiences, I learned how not to deal with people. And, if they want to watch me, and I think they will, I'll show them how to come back from adversity. I'm David. They're Goliath.

A friend and developer from Singapore was very supportive of me. He said, "Don, you are a tall tree. When the wind comes, it will blow the top off, but the trunk will stand. I know you, and I know what you can do." He gave me a 162-site development to manage and sell for him, and he reset my career. This reset to my career allowed me to elevate my business to new heights. I had been selling $150 million worth of property a year when I was with a franchise group; on my own that year with Don Ha Real Estate, I did $750 million. I realized it's people and relationships like this that will allow my business to keep growing.

When RE/MAX approached me to join their franchise group in New Zealand, I didn't make much of it as I was content on my own. But I realized you can only achieve so much on your own.

RE/MAX is a big company—with over 140,000 agents in more than 110 countries and territories. They have a book called *Everyone Wins*, and it says one log of wood makes a lousy fire, and one thousand logs of wood make a great fire. Don Ha Real Estate was that one log (well, maybe a hundred), but "one thousand logs" is when you are part of an international franchise. RE/MAX says to its franchises and agents, "We can take you to the world." And that's what I wanted. Now the world of real estate knows who I am.

Recap and Review

- Good, loyal people are irreplaceable. You need to remember that your people are your best assets. Cultivate the very best and take care of them, and you will be rewarded.

- Sometimes negative circumstances can push you out of your comfort zone. Sometimes when you are backed into a corner, you figure out what you are made of. We all love our comfort zones, but real growth is found outside of them.

- If you do not believe in yourself, why should someone else? When my people returned to help me rebuild, it was because they could look me in the eyes and know that I absolutely had the courage of my convictions. It was insane to think I could buy back my company three weeks after receivership. But I never doubted.

- When you are vulnerable, relationships are strengthened. What seemed like the worst crisis of my life actually showed I was human. It strengthened my bonds with clients and with my own people.

We all need anchors. None of us can do this life without friends and family. Figure out your trusted anchors, and learn to be open with them so that they can offer you their best advice or support.

PART III

RETENTION

CHAPTER 7

DON HA'S PRINCIPLES

OF REAL ESTATE SALES AND INVESTING

Don't wait to buy real estate. Buy real estate and wait.

—WILL ROGERS

P eople approach me all the time at speeches I give or after pre-
sentations—sometimes they even recognize me while I am at a
restaurant or an event. When people wait to talk to me after I
speak, I try to get to every single person wanting a few moments of
my time. Most of them have the same questions: Should I buy real
estate? What's a good real estate investment? What do you think the
market will be doing in the next six months? But the most common
question is, How can I do what you do, Don? They want to know my
secrets of real estate sales, investments, and my ability to do so much,
year after year of progress with so much mental resilience.

I know some people closely guard their "secrets" to sales and
success. I am not like that. I want this book to inspire every single
person who reads it to reach for the stars, and I am happy to share the
wisdom I have accumulated over my career. I intend for this chapter—
and the next one, chapter 8 on my Principles for Life—to be practical,
with actionable steps and ideas you can start doing right now.

Rule Number One: Always Up Your Game

Right now, many Realtors worldwide are panicking! Artificial intelligence (AI) and ChatGPT are frightening people who worry the world is changing too fast. AI may impact or eliminate certain jobs, and Realtors are one profession that the doomsayers claim will go away.

In addition, today it is true that homebuyers often arrive to a home showing or to a meeting with their Realtor having already researched houses themselves, using Zillow or some other real estate app or website. In New Zealand, we use Trade Me and Realestate. co.nz. They often already know which houses they want to tour—or perhaps they even have their house all picked out. They are more discerning and know which features they want. Forty years ago, there were not streaming channels and television shows devoted to real estate, renovating houses, and design. Today's homebuyers are ready with their questions, concerns, and wants. Between this and the rise of AI, some say real estate agents will become obsolete.

You won't see me worried about this. First of all, I firmly believe most people want a human connection. If you doubt that, consider how many people call a business—a bank, a medical practice, an insurance company, or a store—and end up screaming into the phone, "Get me a human! Connect me to customer service!"

This desire for a human connection is even more true when it comes to the biggest purchase of someone's life. It is one thing to use machines or AI like the self-checkout at the grocery store, but it is something else entirely to make a life-changing purchase via a computer and not a person.

Second, we all must accept that technology is here to stay. The Realtors who will excel in real estate now and going forward will be the ones who learn how to use the new tech, apps, and AI to their advantage. They will have an edge over their competitors.

Third, and perhaps most important, you must always up your game. In the reality of today's market, yes, people want a human connection to walk them through the complexities of buying a house. However, you must also be that Realtor who people want to work with because you go above and beyond.

As a real estate agent, what do you offer? Is your knowledge of a property just what is found in the multiple listing service? Do you know about as much as your client could find on real estate platforms?

That is not acceptable. I try to hammer home this point to all my agents. You've got to study the product. Really study it. You must be *the* encyclopedia of that product. Be better than AI! Your product is not just the house but also steering clients through the contracts and fine print, as well as having knowledge of the community where you are selling.

When I represent a property—whether that is selling an entire condominium complex or a single home—I learn everything there is to know about it. This includes

- school districts;
- nearby parks, retail shopping, grocery stores, and restaurants;
- market data;
- safety information (crime rates, etc.);
- home values; and
- potential for re-development.

More importantly, you cannot learn all that online. When I say you must be an encyclopedia, I mean knowing what it is really like to live in that neighborhood and knowing absolutely everything about your property.

I do not believe that real estate professionals will not be needed anymore. How can you tell if the property's been flooded before or if the roof is leaking? AI can't know what the potential of the property is. *I can.* I can apply my decades in the business and all my accumulated knowledge—along with my creative intuition and gut instincts—and provide recommendations to a client. You can obtain basic information via the internet, such as if it's a hundred square meter property. But the internet won't tell you that the land could be developed into commercial property, into a hotel, or other things that machines can't know. It can't tell you about the view or whether young families are anxious to move into the neighborhood because it has the best schools. It can't gather feedback from neighbors either—*you* can.

When you know everything about a community or neighborhood, that expertise is extremely valuable. I found the more I knew, the more successful I became. People seek out experts—especially, again, for the most important decision they will make. It is not only their most expensive purchase but the choice about where they will reside and build a family and a life, the place they will create the dreams they want to enjoy.

I look at it this way: The Apple Watch is a great product. People who own one love it and rely on it. But the Rolex, with its craftsmanship and reputation, is never going to go away, as I am a true collector of Rolex watches. There is always a place for excellence above and beyond. I love the words Rolex uses in their marketing:

> *This is all we make, but we make it all.*
> *So that, in time, you can make it your own.*

> —ROLEX

Provide that excellence.

Rule Number Two: Stay Passionate

I am incredibly lucky in that the career I chose all those years ago is still the one I am excited about each and every day. When you can keep your excitement up, that will lead you to work harder, and you will achieve more success.

Excitement and passion are the fuel to drive the engine of your career.

I had a passion for this business from the first day I learned I could make money talking to people and helping them by their starter homes. I enjoyed everything about real estate and investing, and for me, this was the perfect job.

Perfect job or not, though, if I had to sell the exact same house day after day, I would be bored. We all need to change things up—new suit or outfit, new haircut, new foods to try, new experiences. Real estate sales is no different.

Perhaps your journey into real estate sales is a Career 2.0. Keep in mind what you love about real estate and why you chose it. Whatever your reasoning, you must keep up your excitement. You must go and explore other avenues of your real estate adventure, such as selling high rises or selling to a new group of people (I will admit, e.g., I have a lot of fun selling real estate for members of the All Blacks New Zealand rugby team). Work with the people you enjoy, and try new and inventive marketing approaches, and track the results. Be creative. Keep it fresh and interesting.

For example, I enjoy creating investment sales for clients to amass a property portfolio as a source of income and to create generational wealth for their families. It is genuinely fun for me to change lives through real estate.

Stay excited. Nurture your career like you tend to a garden. Feed and water it. But plant a variety so that you have all sorts of blooms.

Keep it challenging. Stay passionate. Keep your mind stimulated with new people and new real estate deals, and you will not only be successful, but you will feel fulfilled as well.

Rule Number Three: Be Prepared to Live in Your Investment Property

Would you let your aunt, parents, or your own children move into your investment property? If not, then you need to examine your values. Yes, there will always be less expensive properties, but that doesn't mean you try to pass along a damaged or subpar property to an unsuspecting person.

Would you live in it? This one always takes people by surprise. After all, you probably have a place to live and a family home. So why would you need to worry about living in your investment property? However, when you buy an investment property and plan to tie up some of your assets in that property, you need to be prepared to live in it.

By this I mean that all people in real estate need to learn that the industry is cyclical. Sometimes you are fortunate enough to buy at a low point or in a buyer's market—and then list the property in a seller's market by holding on to it for the right amount of time. However, depending on your liquidity, sometimes the wisest course or decision is to sell other properties you have—and move into your investment property.

I once had a couple who wanted financial freedom, for their investments to eventually be their income and to enjoy life through a carefully obtained real estate portfolio. They were very ambitious and wanted to emulate my success, and so I told them to rent their current house and stay with one of their parents for two years in order to save enough to buy a second property or even a third. I even helped them put together a budget. So sometimes, yes, you might have to live in a property you originally earmarked as an investment—or be willing to make sacrifices to build your empire.

In addition, though, it is important to look carefully at that property. If you think to yourself, *I would never live in this dump*, how can you expect anyone to buy it from you? And if you *do* think some desperate person would buy that terrible property, what does it say about how you value your clients?

Rule Number Four: Buy a Property with Land

We live in a very busy society. Townhomes and condominiums where an association takes care of the external elements of the property, as well as the landscaping, are a truly wonderful choice for some. For example, people who travel a great deal often like the fact that a condominium is "turnkey." They can leave without worrying about their apartment too much, and off they go. Homeowners Associations (HOAs) that are *well run* (very important) ensure the properties are well maintained.

Townhouses or condos can sometimes be a first-time buyer's entry into owning real estate. Single-family homes generally cost more than townhomes for the same square footage. However, when it comes to investing, or even getting into your own first home, save a little longer and try to get a property with land.

First of all, homes with land nearly always appreciate faster than townhouses or condominiums. According to my own experience, 80 percent of homebuyers would prefer a free-standing house versus townhouses, condos, or duplexes or triplexes. Reasons vary. For instance, you certainly have more privacy in a house versus sharing a wall with a neighbor. A home with land can afford young families a backyard for kids to play in. However, this 80 percent figure is very important. When you go to sell or resell a single-family house, the pool of eager buyers will be much larger than for a condo.

However, it is always better to start somewhere in your real estate journey. So, if a condominium is what you can afford, just get your foot in the investment/real estate door. Then trade up!

In addition, as you grow in your exponential success, if you buy a property with enough land, you can become a developer and build an additional house (or more) on the available land you own.

Land is king. (Or queen!)

Rule Number Five: Check Out the Neighborhood—Carefully

I mentioned earlier, you must be a walking, talking encyclopedia of a property. I also said it is important for you to check out properties in person. I am going to give you an example of this rule—with a mistake I made. I purchased a house in a rough area with a high level of crime. I thought I'd just snap up this property at a bargain, fix it up properly, and sell it. My lawyer was brought up in that area, and he even cautioned me not to buy it. He said the neighborhood had issues with crime and vandalism. But I was young and thought I knew it all, and I went and bought this run-down house anyway despite the fact that I am not a house flipper. There is nothing wrong with that approach, but as you can see from this book, I am a long-term investor and developer. I play the long game.

That was the worst house I ever bought because the house got broken into every week. I had visions of replacing the appliances, painting every wall clean and neutral, painting the outside, and making it a lovely starter home for someone. At every step of the renovation, graffiti was sprayed on the walls. Vandals even took the stove and the hot water cylinder.

I sold it for a loss.

Thus, it's very important to buy the right property, in the right location, and to thoroughly check out the neighborhood. Ask the people who live around the street to see what the neighborhood is like. In addition, if you choose to buy a home that is empty in a neighborhood, having good relations with the neighbors is important. They can keep an eye on the property until you sell it or someone moves in.

Remember, the human touch is something AI has not mastered. Talk to people. Reach out. Ask questions.

It's also not just neighborhoods that might have vandalism. The most beautiful homes can have issues too. For example, I have seen properties where there is a right of way to the beach. Everyone in the neighborhood understands that is the access and all honor and respect the access drive. But now a new neighbor with a wild lifestyle has parties every single weekend. Not only is there noise and too much traffic on a residential street—their guests are parking ten cars in the right of way. Now the neighborhood is fractured—not only is access a problem, but there is conflict as well.

Now, after I had grown a little older—and a lot wiser—I had a win in an auction of distressed properties where I knew what I was taking on. Our competition was bidding on the houses too, but I won eleven out of twelve properties.

At the auction, they stopped me at four homes—literally paused the auction. They said, "Where's your money?" And I replied, "It's in my pocket." I had my checkbook.

Ah, but here's the secret to that deal. I wrote a check, but before it was even deposited in the bank, I had investors for every single house lined up, and I made money on the transaction. I knew the neighborhood was on the upswing and that these houses would make great investments.

Rule Number Six: Be Sure of Your Finances—and Watch the Numbers

I am sure every single person reading this book has heard the real estate advice: "Don't fall in love with a house."

This refers to when you go to buy *your* home. Of course, you want to love the house you buy, especially if you think of it as your forever home and it has features you want, such as an upgraded kitchen or a showstopping entranceway. What the expression means is do not love a house so much that you ignore warning signs that it perhaps is not the best investment or purchase. Your love of the house overtakes common sense.

The same idea can apply to real estate investment. The following scenario is one I have seen. Someone purchases a townhome as an investment property because they cannot quite swing the bigger price of a single-family home. They look at the price tag of the townhome, and it's really a stretch, and the value and the numbers are razor-thin margin. However, they are anxious to be an investor. They ignore the numbers and think they can make it work because they feel certain the rent on the property will pay the mortgage, but they have no wiggle room.

Say they have bought the townhouse for $800,000. They have a mortgage of $700,000 after putting $100,000 down (and I am using these numbers for illustrative purposes only—I know $100,000 is a lot of money for most people!). They are planning on the rental paying for the remainder of the mortgage terms. However, there really is no buffer budget—for repairs one day, or the potential months between renters, or even a problem renter who is late on payments.

Next these investors will say, "It's not paying for itself, but I can offset my taxes against it." They continue to kid themselves about the investment and its value.

In theory, that taxation idea might work, but it really does not because of the lack of breathing room in their numbers. Worse, if the investor loses their day job, suddenly they cannot make payments on the property. In their current crisis, they are more concerned about keeping their primary residence.

Then they can lose it all.

You must study your numbers, do the math, and make smart decisions. Don't fall in love with the idea of real estate investing any more than you should fall in love with a house.

Rule Number Seven: Do Ten by Ten—and Five Hundred

You may remember I touched on ten calls by ten—and contacting five hundred people. I put them here as Rule Number Seven for one reason: they are nonnegotiable.

Every person who is reading this book is being given a road map for exponential success. Not everyone will follow this plan, but I promise you the successful ones will.

So, remember, one of the recommendations I give when new agents come to work for me is to make ten personal phone calls by ten in the morning. Not emails. Not texts. Phone calls establish rapport, trust, and deepen a relationship with potential buyers.

Often, when I tell people this idea of ten-by-ten is very important, they ask, "Well, what do I say to these ten people if they aren't in the market for a house?"

In fact, that is the point. Real estate sales is about *relationships*, not the hard sell. You can't force someone to buy a house or list it with you. But you can make sure they know they can call on you when the time does come for them to make a real estate decision because you have built trust with them.

A ten-by-ten call doesn't have to be about real estate. After a while, these types of calls will be easy for you. This is a very simple concept and should not fill you with anxiety. "I just called to touch base with you, and to see how you are. ... How is your family? ... Oh, new grandchild—that's wonderful news."

It's *conversation*—not salesmanship.

Now, because of how far I have come in real estate, some people are actually a little flattered that I have called them personally. Here I have had over a billion dollars in real estate listings, but I *still* make the time to make ten calls before ten.

(Oh, and a little secret—sometimes I make those calls before nine. As long as you are not calling at dawn, what is the difference between 8:45 and 9:00 in the morning?)

The next "must do" rule is five hundred—a number you must remember. Five hundred what? Business cards. In your first ninety days, give out five hundred cards—give them to everyone you know and a few you don't! Talk to everyone you meet.

Now, I already know about half the people reading this book (maybe more) will say, "Don, I don't even *know* five hundred people. I can't possibly give out five hundred cards in three months."

Imagine if I challenged you: Here's a hundred thousand dollars. I want you to throw yourself the most spectacular birthday party ever. Invite every single person you know. You can have it at this fabulous hotel on the water—the highest quality food and drinks, music, decorations. Just splurge and make it the best party anyone has ever attended. *But the catch is you can't have even 499 attendees.* You must invite five hundred.

I promise you, your guest list would have five hundred people on it. You'd literally run through everyone you've ever been friends with, hung out with, and their brothers and sisters and parents too!

You'd look up old teachers and neighbors and coworkers. You would be able to get your list up to that. Just start a list as an exercise—you may be surprised!

Yet when I tell people to make contact with five hundred people to launch their real estate career—a pathway to financial freedom and wealth—they will say, "I can maybe think of twenty-five or thirty people I can call, invite for coffee, and give one of my cards to."

How badly do you want exponential success? If you want it badly enough, you will do this step. Remember, when I was knocking on doors and trying to sell houses in my first year, my accent and my background defied conventional wisdom of who can be successful. If I could give out all those cards and talk to all those people, you can too.

Rule Number Eight: Dress and Act the Part

If you were going to put your life savings down on a house, who would you rather buy it from? A sloppy person in jeans and a T-shirt? Or the person in professional clothes, with a suit, a fresh haircut, or wearing a beautiful dress or pantsuit, the person, in other words, put together and looking sharp?

We all know the answer.

In my offices, every single person dresses as if they were the CEO of a successful company. In a way, my people are. They are each the CEO of their own success, and they look and dress the part accordingly.

I can tell you that when you walk into my building—the one with my name on the side in big letters—you are going to be offered tea or coffee. You will be greeted by the most professional-looking Realtors in New Zealand. They will greet you warmly. They will impress you. I want every person who works with us to look around and think, "Wow, this is a successful company, and I can put my trust in these people."

I will add respectful manners—your actions should reflect positively on you, the agency where you work, and your profession. Impeccable manners and respect are things I insist on in my company.

Rule Number Nine: Be Sure of the Valuation

Obviously, most real estate transactions involve negotiations. Someone bids a price, you offer them a lower price, and ideally you meet in the middle. It is essential for any real estate investor, though, to know the valuation of a house. If a house is overvalued, you just lost money as soon as you closed. If a house is undervalued, you may have just made 10 or 20 percent on your investment—without doing a thing.

Valuation becomes extremely important in volatile economic times. If you overpay by even as little as 10 percent, and then the market has a downturn of, say, 20 percent, you lose all the capital gains you had anticipated.

It is extremely important in real estate not to indulge in magical thinking. If you are talking yourself into a purchase, listen very carefully to the "logical" voice inside. Wishing and hoping for a valuation to go up when you have already overpaid is not sensible investing.

I also have to add that you don't actually *lose* money until you sell it at a lower price than what you paid. Sometimes, you need to be prepared to hold on to an investment property until the market rises again.

Rule Number Ten: Go Where the Money Is

During the pandemic I bought a million-dollar home off the internet. The property was an hour and a half flight from Auckland. Now, you might think after Rule Number Nine that a decision like that sounds very risky. However, we were in lockdown, which meant I could not go to see it in person except for from the outside.

However, I was watching the market, and the house had an inspection (so I was certain there were no hidden surprises awaiting me—such as a leaky roof or a bad heating, ventilating, and air-conditioning [HVAC] system), and I knew that the neighborhood and the area were excellent. I have also honed my judgment over the years. I knew this home was a good value, and I knew even though it cost more than a million dollars, this beautiful home would rise in value.

I did not intend to live in the house. I was following the money—where real estate values were rising. Fifteen months later, I sold it for over double the price I paid.

You may be comfortable being a Realtor in a certain area, but if it is not an area of growth, you will be limiting the level of success you can obtain. If it is a stagnant neighborhood, or at a low price point, it will be tough to advance in your career. You must follow the energy and go where there is money to be made.

A perfect example is Australia's Gold Coast. Predictions are that the area will outperform all other states in Australia. It is a highly desirable area. Watching what's happening along the Gold Coast, I will be investing there. In fact, I analyze markets around the world, and this enables me to buy properties in locations that are growing and to hold on to properties in markets that are slowing down until they are on the upswing again. You'll hear more in the next chapter about how I am even intending on investing in Vietnam—the country of my birth.

Rule Number Eleven: You Don't Have to Work for Your Money

Sometimes, you don't need to work harder for your money; you need to work smarter.

I remember about twenty years ago, I was reading the paper, and there was a small print ad for two acres of land on a beautiful mountain peak for $500,000. The views were spectacular, and good views are always something homebuyers want.

I went to meet the landowner, and I asked him, "Why are you selling such a beautiful piece of property?"

Straightaway, he told me his business was in trouble. I asked him, "How much money do you need right now?"

He replied $20,000. I said, "I will give you $20,000 right now, and then another $20,000 in two months"—which is when he needed more. Over six months, I would buy this land.

A year later, this land was worth $750,000 because of a rise in the market.

So, you don't always need to work harder—just smarter. You can make money by giving people what they want—I helped him keep his business afloat, and I got what I wanted (the land), and it was a win-win. I still read the print paper every weekend—because you never know what might be lurking there as an opportunity. Often the good deals are in the fine print.

Think outside the box—be clever, read people, care about people. Look at deals from all different angles. Work smarter.

Rule Number Thirteen: Make Sure You Can Trust Your Realtor

This may seem like a strange thing for a very successful Realtor and CEO to say, however, you need to realize that real estate professionals are human. They make mistakes. Some are better at the real estate game than others. Not every real estate professional is trustworthy. For some, they may be unscrupulous. Or they may simply be very new.

A huge mistake people make is walking into a Realtor's office and assuming every person there is qualified to be their Realtor. This is an especially important warning if you are getting into investing—which has more legal and financial complexities. I advise asking questions including:

- How long have you been in business?

- How many properties have you sold?

- Do you own any investment property yourself?

If they don't have investment property experience, then how can they advise you? So, the next questions would be the following: "Do you know anyone in your office who sells investment property? Can I meet that agent? Can I talk to them?" Then the new agent can sit with the experienced agent and listen to their advice, which I do with all my agents. They get to sit in on my meetings so that they can not only listen to my advice but also get to know how I interact with my clients.

In fact, recently I brought two new Realtors with me as I negotiated for an exclusive on two large subdivisions. I have them listen and learn—see how it's done!

An investor who wants to spend $800,000 on a property cannot just walk in and talk to someone who just started out in real estate, doesn't know anything about the property, and doesn't know about the finance side of such a transaction.

New real estate agents tend to focus on selling their first properties. They are eager, and sometimes they may be in over their head. This is why I mentor my agents. It is important they learn the ropes before they give advice to investors.

Rule Number Fourteen: It's Not Always About the Sale

It's not about the sale. It's about two words: *trust* and *respect*. Those two words are the pillars of my business.

Remember Rule Number Seven—where I encouraged you to make ten calls by ten. Those calls are not hard-sell calls. They are relationship-building calls.

Not making every encounter about the sale is one of my important principles. You are building trust with the person you are selling real estate to. I never make a sale on my first visit with someone. This is one of the secrets to my success. It's not about the hard sell.

How can I find the perfect home for someone, as I have countless times, if I don't speak with them, listen to what it is they truly want, and if I don't care about *them* but only my own pocket and the sale? I have literally visited properties, walked in, and have known *precisely* which of my clients would love everything about it. The delight on their faces when I take them to tour the property is worth all my hard work over the years. It's still a thrill to make people happy.

Making every relationship about the sale is totally the wrong attitude. I will give an example I have seen happen. A new buyer trusts a Realtor who is all about the sale. With only that sale in mind, the Realtor does not negotiate a good price. Perhaps the buyer loves the house (breaking the rule about "Don't fall in love with the house," but sometimes it's hard not to!). The Realtor knows the buyer will simply pay asking price or above asking price—even when there is negotiation room.

If you continue to look after yourself and not the buyer and oversell the properties you close on, after six months, what if the buyer's circumstances change? More than once, I have received a call not all that long after closing, saying, "Hey, Don, I need to sell my house now because my husband passed away [or I lost my job or I'm moving overseas]."

I provide the right advice, the truth about future potential, and by the way, I do that for both sides. Sometimes I represent the buyer. Sometimes the seller. Either way, I am honest and ensure my clients' trust is not misplaced.

These principles have enabled me to have a long and fruitful career in real estate. However, they are not my only rules. I also have principles for life, and they are essential to success too. Life is meant to be lived with principles—your character and the trust you build are the real reasons your clients put their faith in you.

CHAPTER 8

DON HA'S PRINCIPLES
FOR LIFE

Watch your thoughts; they become words.
Watch your words; they become actions.
Watch your actions; they become habits.
Watch your habits; they become character.
Watch your character; it becomes your destiny.

—LAO-TZE

I think a successful life is one in which you make a difference. Why are we here? I would say it's not only for us to live a happy and successful life, an honorable life, but also for us to change the lives of the people around us. To leave the people we encounter better somehow for having met us.

Before I tell you my principles for life, I have a special story.

As a first-generation immigrant—one who went through extreme hardship and even hunger—I know the people who gave me chances in my life are very important. That first person, and the second person, who bought a house from me when I was starting out. The people who bought my watercress. The martial arts instructor who chose me to lead the class. Consequently, I believe in giving people chances. I also believe in second chances.

In fact, I was a guest speaker at a prison—hoping to inspire them to lead new lives once they were released. As I drove onto the grounds of Spring Hill Corrections Facility, I saw low-lying white buildings with red-clay-colored roofs spread across the vibrant green grounds. But I also saw the guard towers, and when I walked into the lobby, it had that institutional smell and polished concrete floors. For a brief moment, I may even have said to myself, "Don, what did you sign up for?"

After passing through security, I was led to a large classroom-like room. There were no bars between me and the thirty or so men I was asked to speak with. They were all very large men—who clearly worked out with weights in the prison exercise yard.

The warden warned me. "Put your sunglasses away. They love sunglasses. They'll steal them!"

I slipped my Ray-Bans in my shirt pocket and walked in. Some of the inmates were Māori, with tattoos on their faces and arms. They were a bit intimidating.

Then, these prisoners performed a haka to welcome me. I felt their stomping feet and very loud, shouted greeting in my stomach— almost like butterflies. I got quite emotional as this was a deep honor. In all my experiences, this had not happened to me—a personal haka.

After they were through, I started talking with them—back and forth, not lecturing. I asked some of them, "Where are you from?" And believe it or not, several of these prisoners were from the same working-class suburb where I lived when I first came to New Zealand—South Auckland.

I asked, "What street?"

Prisoners called out, "I lived on this street," "I lived on that street."

One of them actually grew up on the exact same street I had—and went to the same school but a decade behind me. I could see they were impressed—someone from the same area, not born with a silver spoon in his mouth but self-made, had achieved exponential success.

This shared background in Otara bonded us. It was no longer "Don Ha" and a room full of prisoners but a conversation. They impressed me with their appreciation and forthrightness, and I said, "To be honest with you guys, when you come out of this prison, society does not want to know you because you have a prison record."

A mistake—often a youthful mistake—was going to limit their opportunities in life and their chances for success. I knew because of that it would be tempting for some of them to return to the streets—the same errors in judgment that sent them to prison in the first place. I counseled them, "But you can change your position in society by going to work for a company."

I knew for some of these men, that would be difficult. Not everyone believes in second chances. But I also felt if they were honest and willing to work hard and learn, someone would offer them an opportunity—it would just be more challenging to get that foot in the door.

"If you can't get a job," I said, "tell the hiring person, 'Look, I'll work for nothing for you. If I produce and do a good job, after you see how hard I will work, then you can offer me a job.'"

Then I offered some words of advice on setting yourself up to succeed in business of any sort:

"The number-one rule is if you do get a job, go to work one hour earlier than everyone else and go home one hour later. Work harder than anyone else there. Don't complain. Apply yourself. Prove your worth. You will get the job then. You can change your life by doing that. Otherwise, honestly, society does not want to offer you a chance to redeem yourselves."

I was quite blunt—because they were in prison ... they certainly did not need me to sugarcoat things. Then I told them my own story, from fleeing Vietnam, through the dark times in Hong Kong, to coming someplace new with no money and not even speaking the language.

"Look, I come from the street where you come from. Look at me today." I tried to think of a tangible sign of success. Then I lifted my wrist and showed them my gold Rolex. I said, "Look, now I'm wearing a Rolex." Smiling, I took it off and ... boom. I threw it out to one of them in the room (thankfully he caught it!), and they passed it around the room. Several of them turned the watch over in their palm, marveling at it.

I am sure the warden thought, *If I told you to hide your sunglasses, why are you passing around a Rolex?*

However, I respected these men, and I felt they respected me—as shown by the haka. Our conversation deepened until it seemed like I had become their best friend. They related to me because I was a poor boy from their hood. I was told I would not succeed—just as they had been. From start to finish, it was one of the most amazing experiences I've had in my life.

That's my "superpower"—I want to change lives. By talking to everyone I meet with respect and with openness, I believe that I make connections that people carry with them after we part. I can get right down to that authentic level and advise a prisoner what to do when they come out. If they deserve a second chance, why doesn't everybody else deserve a second chance or an opportunity?

I have given former prisoners jobs with my company after they have served their debt to society. However, this book is about exponential success, and you can only achieve that if you do the work.

I also want to tell you an opposite story about another prisoner. He wrote to me from behind bars. I wrote back, and I sent him a real estate book that I wrote in the year 2000. I don't ignore people who reach out.

When this man was released from prison, he looked me up and phoned me. He said, "Remember me? You sent me a book when I was in prison and asked you for advice on going into real estate."

I did recall him. We chatted, and at that time, he was very fond of racehorses—he had read in the papers about my investments in horses. We had a pleasant conversation.

I invited him out to my farm and showed him some of my horses. I drove us to the farm, and I remember the ride out there; he was very impressed with my shoes of all things. Jokingly, I thought, *Well, if prisoners did not steal my Rolex, they're not going to steal my shoes.*

We had a wonderful afternoon, and I advised him how he could break into real estate. But I never heard from him again.

If you are offered a chance, you have to take it. No one can do it for you.

When I set out to write this book, aside from real estate advice, I knew that I had some life lessons that could be applied to people from all walks of life, all different experiences. I call these my Principles for Life.

Number One: Never Forget Where You Came From

As you can tell from my story, I hold this rule close to my heart. My childhood and all I experienced made me who I am today. You cannot separate Don Ha from his childhood. My experiences mean I appreciate where I am today. My experiences mean I work harder than anyone else.

By not forgetting where I came from, I also ensure I remain humble. I remember what it was like to not be given a chance, for people to assume things about me because of my accent or my background as a refugee. I remember my mother's sadness at not having fresh food to cook for us in Hong Kong—and as a boy doing something about that.

We all know people who "make it"—and promptly forget where they came from and the people who were integral to their success. I am reminded of movie stars who set out to become famous, and as soon as they do, they complain they have no privacy. That attitude will never be me. I enjoy having nice things—fancy cars, a Rolex, a magnificent water view from my clifftop home, traveling to amazing places, and taking vacations with my family. However, I am still Don Ha, the boy collecting dented cans to sell them for fresh vegetables.

The Oscar-winning movie *Everything Everywhere All at Once* depicts a metaverse in which the characters exist across multiple universes— same characters, different lives. In some ways, that reminds me of this rule for life. I am *this* Don Ha, a CEO, a successful entrepreneur. I am also the Don Ha who left everything he knew for a terrifying voyage across the sea to a refugee camp. He is inside me too. I am both of them at all times, and it has given me a unique perspective on life, which I am so grateful I have been able to share with you.

Number Two: Look for Challenges

Some of us get comfortable. We make a good income, take our family on vacation once a year, and sort of hover there—right in the middle. We are not falling backward. But we're not pushing forward either. We might even be stagnant.

I think challenges keep us growing. They force us to expand our mind, heart, and spirit. For me, challenges are my life fuel. I thrive on difficulties. I always recall my father saying, "Watching you gives me a headache. Why can't you be happy with where you are?"

What he doesn't understand is that solving those knotty problems is what makes me happy. Give me a challenge, and I will try to figure out a path to success. Helping others solve their challenges also gives me satisfaction.

I also have challenged myself at every step of my career. We hear so much today about "gamifying" our ambitions—I've been doing that for many years. By that I mean that throughout my journey, if someone told me, "The top earner earned $250,000 in commissions last year," I immediately would say, "Great. I will make $500,000."

As I grew my real estate portfolio, it eventually became time to have my own office. That was my next challenge—and happily I passed the test with flying colors. Then, all these years later, I'm the regional owner and CEO of RE/MAX New Zealand and Fiji.

Wanting challenges is *not* the same thing as being ungrateful or dissatisfied. I love my life and appreciate it all—from my team (which I will discuss later in the chapter) to my family and friends, to my beautiful home, and all of the exciting experiences I get to enjoy.

But I still like a challenge. I enjoy figuring out solutions that no one else sees. Only through stretching and pushing ourselves will we reach exponential success.

Number Three: Family above All Else

I know a wealthy businessman—worth a lot of money, with all the trappings of success. He is on his fourth wife, and he has multiple children from his previous wives—kids he doesn't see all that often. We all know people who are successful in their careers—but not relationships.

It is easy to forget a marriage or relationship as you are building your empire or your fortune and you're putting in those long, long hours. You must not lose sight of the people important to you.

For me, it is family. Part of the secret to my success is having a true partner in my wife. Smart, beautiful, supportive, an amazing mother—she is the whole package as they say. I truly could not do what I do without knowing that my children and our lives are cared for. Someone has to make sure our household runs smoothly, ensure we all have what we need for success—whether that is me in my career or my children in school. (And my children are all on paths to be entrepreneurs—even from a young age.)

I believe I was fortunate to meet my wife as I found a true partner. Partners communicate. They allow each other the space to be successful in what they do. But they are a *team*. My wife and I may not agree with each other on everything (wouldn't that be boring?), but we are both working for the same goals. We don't lose sight of them. She respects and trusts my decisions on our investments and my career, and I respect and trust her decisions on our lives and our children's lives.

I have also ensured that my parents, siblings, and other family are all cared for—I've guided them to millionaire status.

Real estate is my passion; family is my purpose.

Number Four: Show Respect at All Times

Respect is something that is as essential to my life as breathing. I insist on it in my company—from the receptionist to my franchise owners to our individual brokers. If you are not respectful, you would not be comfortable working for me. I talked about this in the last chapter. But it's so important that I add it here as a Rule for Life, too. Because you may be a Realtor for ten hours a day, but you are a human for twenty-four.

I also insist that people respect my team—I don't care who you are. For example, an investor with many, many millions of dollars came into our office and berated my staff, spoke rudely to our receptionist, and behaved, frankly, horribly. I phoned him after his visit and said, "You were disrespectful to my people, and it doesn't matter how much money you have. You will not be doing business with me."

Consider how you show respect to others. At Don Ha Real Estate, every person entering our office is greeted and made to feel welcome. I have had many brokers join our team over the years who have said they wanted to work for me because of the culture of our organization. I remember one woman telling me, "Everyone is so happy here. There's no tension in this office—it's so warm and positive."

Another example is that in my company, if you invite people to lunch, you had better pay. If I take five people to lunch with me, I will pay the tab. But I will also expect my people to reciprocate at some point. Call it hospitality or respect, but I feel it is much classier and demonstrates appreciation. We don't split the checks.

I will notice behaviors that do not demonstrate respect. For example, as I've told you, I make ten calls by ten o'clock every morning. Those are not sales calls but touching base calls, the "I just called to say hello and see how you are" type calls. Yet, time and again, as I have grown more successful, there are some people over the years who would never call me to ask about me, my family, life in general. Instead, they only phone me when they want something.

I will never forget helping a young family get into their first home—I had worked a budget with them and advised them. They wanted me to see their house once they were moved in. I arrived at their house, and per the cultural customs, I went to remove my shoes in the foyer upon entering the house. This is a sign of respect for someone's home in certain cultures.

"No, Don!" They insisted. "Do not take off your shoes. This is your house too! No need."

I was touched by their respect and esteem for me, and I told them, "No. This is *your* house now." I was so happy to see them in their home, building their new lives.

Respect for everyone is one of the most important themes of success.

Number Five: Pay It Forward

Success allows you to share. I don't mean money (though sharing that is fun, too). I mean wisdom and mentorship. When you achieve your goals, don't forget the journey and your struggles. Be sure to take new people in your field under your wing.

In my company, there are no side deals. I have had experienced Realtors come to me wanting to join my company. They often have a list of what they want—including their own compensation plan and side transactions. Part of paying it forward, for me, is ensuring everyone has an equal opportunity. My team succeeds together—we don't tolerate backstabbing.

Whether it is speaking at prisons or speaking at a conference or giving a keynote speech, I will speak with everyone who wants to after my talk. Sometimes the line is pretty long, but it is worth it for me to offer some words of encouragement to the people waiting to meet me. If someone is new to real estate or considering a career switch, I am happy to speak with them. I also enjoy meeting the sons and daughters of colleagues and friends and giving them some guidance on how to get ahead in real estate—and life.

One recent experience was very special in this regard. I was traveling in India when I entered a Louis Vuitton store. I got to speaking with the manager. She grew animated when I told her about my sales career and handed her my card. She then asked if I would speak to her sales team. She actually closed early, locked the doors, and I proceeded to tell them my story, where I am today, and some of my secrets to sales. They were so appreciative, and that spur-of-the-moment encounter made me so happy to pass along some of my knowledge to a group of eager, young salespeople.

This book, I hope, has demonstrated to you that there is not a finite amount of success in the world—it's there for everyone for the taking. Consequently, there is simply no need to be stingy with your time and advice.

Paying it forward, to me, is the cost of being a human on this crowded planet.

Number Six: Watch Your Habits

Bad habits are not conducive to success. They can be simple negative habits—sleeping in, eating only junk food, too many late-night parties. But bad habits also crop up in business behaviors. Maybe you start letting your business "run itself" instead of tending to it, or you don't compensate your employees fairly and have huge turnover.

I will never forget a dinner I attended with six other very successful businesspeople and investors. They were all drinking whiskey, stepping outside to smoke cigars, and so on. One of them joked, "We better watch it. Don Ha doesn't drink and we're all here drinking—he's at 100 percent. We're not."

Of course, the others around the table laughed. But I thought to myself, *If you only knew how true that is.* I want to be at 100 percent all the time.

If you want to have exponential success, watch your habits. If you think you have a problem, go get help.

Number Seven:
The Buck Stops with You

I would never want to paint a picture that everything in my world always goes perfectly and that every single agent who works for me is always the best. We try to hire the highest quality people in the entire industry, but when you are at a large corporation with many franchises and employees, it is not possible for every person to be perfect. Some will make mistakes.

Fairly recently, I received a furious phone call from a large developer who was going to cancel our exclusive contract to sell his properties. This contract was worth a great deal of money, and even if it hadn't been, I do not like unhappy clients.

I was stunned, and I asked him for a meeting. Prior to the meeting, I did some investigating, and my agent had cut corners. He was being lazy, and he was simply not doing his job the way I taught him, and the way I expected as his CEO. It was, simply put, not the Don Ha way.

I went to the meeting with humility and honesty. I said to the developer:

"I discovered that my employee did not take care of you the way he should have. He didn't follow the plan I outlined for him, and I had no idea this was going on. I truly apologize for this. There are no excuses—not with me. I trusted him, but regardless, *my* reputation is on the line. If you give me a chance, I will personally oversee this and ensure you get the results you want and deserve. I personally guarantee this. The buck stops with me."

This man gave me and my company another chance. There are actually three lessons hidden in this little story. The first is that honesty, humility, respect, and ethics will always be a winning strategy. If he *hadn't* given my company the chance to make it right, it would still be a winning strategy because I did not compromise my principles. I accepted the responsibility for the mistakes made by my team.

Two, if I hadn't cultivated a real relationship and the trust that entails, I would never have been given that chance. I had a strong foundation with this client that I had worked to build over time.

The third is that the buck always needs to stop with you—no excuses. If you are a real estate agent, or are in any profession, be honest when mistakes happen—and be transparent. People appreciate the truth. If you are a leader, it's even more important to embody this rule. Don't blame your employees. Instead, figure out a way to make things right.

Number Eight: Create Your Team— and Take Care of Them

When I went through the ordeal of the receivership, I learned who my true friends were. Some people expressed sympathy to my face but tried to hire my people away from me or participated in gossip. I also learned who my most loyal employees were. It is difficult to articulate how meaningful it was for most of them to tell me they were going to stand by me—that they believed in me and trusted me. I am sure they were shocked at just how quickly I bounced back—or maybe not! Maybe they weren't surprised because they had so much faith in me.

All along in my company, I have sought to hire the very best. Some of them may arrive to interview with very little or no experience, but if I sense the *passion,* that cannot be taught. I want those who wake up excited to work hard and to create a lasting impact, to sell real estate and make people's dreams come true by finding them their ideal home. Those are the agents I want to have as part of the Don Ha family.

I've always prided myself on being generous with my agents— even very recently raising their compensation as I said earlier in the chapter. However, I have been burned a few times. I've loaned money and have not been repaid, or I have been fooled by a sad story that turned out to be false. However, I refuse to be cynical. I may be more *careful* than I used to be with people as my success has grown, but I refuse to let negative experiences change me at my core.

Your team is also not just your work team, though. Your team is also your family, your trusted advisers or mentors, the people in your circle you can count on. I have friends outside of real estate whom I like to bounce things off—it's a small circle, but they are part of my support team nonetheless.

Be cautious about who you let on your team. Choose them carefully. But when you have your team assembled, ensure you take care of them.

Number Nine: Be True to Yourself

The Don Ha you would meet today is not all that different from the Don Ha when I started out in real estate. I have remained true to who I am.

Now, my circumstances have certainly changed. The boy who collected watercress to make ends meet is not the man who wears a Rolex and gives speeches to hundreds of people, who has sold billions of dollars in real estate.

But I am still the same.

I still live to work hard. I would not know what it is like to not be problem solving, selling, mentoring, networking, leading workshops, or traveling to meetings—all of it keeps me energized.

I still look out for my family and want to make their lives better. I still mentor young people and new agents. I still make those ten-by-ten calls, no matter how "big" I have gotten in the real estate world.

I still like to help people and make a difference.

As I said in Rule One about not forgetting where you came from, I am the principled Don Ha in any metaverse! I can look around and see many successful people succumb to their wealth—I word it like that because their wealth changes them, and they lose who they once were. Remain true to yourself on this journey. What is the point of success if you lose your soul in the process?

Number Ten: Think Bigger

This rule is so important. (They all are! It was difficult to decide what order to put them in. I don't want you to think that since this one is Number Ten, it is less important than Number One. They all work together to create exponential success. I am giving you the secret formula.) You must think bigger and bolder.

I notice when I interview people for jobs in my company, I often think their aspirations and determination are not big enough. I always ask them, "How much money do you want to make? What are your ambitions?"

Some will say, "I want to make $75,000 a year." And that's nice. But not big enough. I have yet to see someone enter my office and say, "I want to make a million dollars." And that's the sad part, because we've been programmed to think that we can't do it. *That the goal is too audacious, and who are we to say that aloud?*

Occasionally, I will interview someone and they tell me, "I want to be you."

I don't laugh at this goal—I encourage it. However, I am very frank—they need both that crazy, big "reach" goal matched with very big determination. I say, "Well, you want to be me, huh? This is what you will need to do."

We take their financial goal for the first year of real estate sales. Let's say they want to make $250,000. We break it down to a monthly and then weekly program of what they have to do. Next we look at where they need to be at six months, at a year, and then we go to two years. By then, they should have been able to purchase some property as well. From that point, we set up a five-year target and then ten years. And they should be millionaires and beyond.

Perhaps you are thinking, *That's too simple. It's not that easy.* In fact, it *is* that simple, but it's not that easy.

If you want to achieve big things, then you need to be willing to do the hard work to get there. This same principle applies to any goal in your life. If you wake up tomorrow and want to run a marathon, you are going to have to put in hard work and training to get across the finish line.

I would say for every one hundred people I interview, there will be one or two who will make it to the millionaire rank. That is no accident. That is not "luck." They are the ones who come in reaching for the stars. And they make their own luck!

Also, did you notice that this rule says "think big," whereas most people will tell you to "dream big"? That is because, one, thinking implies not just dreaming up a goal but thinking it through. Second, once you have a dream and you achieve it, then what? All along you should be thinking bigger and bigger, planning and focusing. Dreams are nice, but they can be like trying to grasp fog in your fingers.

Think big. It will make your plans more concrete.

Number Eleven: There Are No Shortcuts

I know it can sound unheard of to make a plan to become a millionaire—and to be given an exact road map to get there from someone who has done it. Whatever your goals in life, if you are lucky enough to have a mentor who is giving you that map, know there are no shortcuts.

I have watched—too many times to count—as people follow my plan. I literally show them exactly what to do. Then they start getting excited. "Oh my goodness, I am making more money than I ever have in my life."

That is the time to double down and keep the momentum going!

However, I have then watched them decide they don't have to work quite so hard. Or they leave my company and go off on their own, certain they now have the secret and can take a shortcut to a franchise or the next level in real estate.

The biggest mistake that all these people have made is they've been on the highway. We're driving in a nice, straight lane. We have the road map. We're going at a fine speed. And then they think, *There's a shortcut to this road.* They reroute, cut through town, and then realize there is a massive traffic jam. So, they have to reverse course and get back on the highway. When we teach these new people for the first one or two years, they think, *Wow, I know it all now.* So, they detour off the highway. Stick to the highway. That's it. It is that simple.

Number Twelve: Remove Fear

Fear will hold you back in your life and career. If I can survive a journey in a boat full of refugees and escape the hardships of the refugee camps and all my experiences—and had the courage of my convictions and ambitions—you can too.

Too many of us think, *What if …?* and we follow that thought with the worst possible outcome. What if I fail? What if I embarrass myself trying something new? What if everyone tells me "no"?

I knocked on so many doors when I was starting out. If I got a "no," then I told myself it was the law of averages. No, no, no, and sooner or later, a yes.

The question you should be asking is "What if I am a huge success? What if I achieve my big dream?"

Fear paralyzes us. We become its prisoner. It grows, becomes bigger than us, and becomes the bars that keep us stuck where we are. We are no less free than the men I visited at Spring Hill Corrections Facility.

Number Thirteen: Watch What You Feed Your Mind

We live in a consuming culture, and one of the things we consume is data and information. We relentlessly scroll on our phones to the point where we don't always interact with the people around us, including our own families.

Some of the content we consume is helpful, but a lot of it is the equivalent of mental junk food. If you want exponential success, you must carefully guard your brain. Feed it healthy food—not junk.

When I was a young man, trying to make my way as a refugee in a strange new place, I took martial arts for the discipline and confidence it instilled in me. I also listened to every motivational tape I could get my hands on. I started with the original master of motivation—Zig Ziglar. That man has inspired generations of achievers. After Zig, I moved on to other great speakers, people who inspired me, who helped me believe in myself and reinforced the success goals and principles I envisioned for myself.

Cut out the junk food in your life—the hateful comments underneath online articles, insipid television shows with little redeeming value, celebrity gossip, or just mindless scrolling without purpose. Instead fill your mind with the healthiest inspiration you can find.

Go to seminars and conferences. See your motivational icons in person if you can. Soak up the energy. Be inspired.

Be careful of the people you surround yourself with too. Are they upbeat people feeding your mind positive energy? Or are they the Debbie Downers, the pessimists of the world? Seek out those who feed your mind—people who believe in you and what you are trying to achieve.

Number Fourteen: Don't Follow the Rules, but Don't Break Them

I love being a trailblazer. If there is something new going on in real estate, I want in. I want to lead the way. I am able to make quick decisions and act on them.

One example I'll give was a recent trip to Las Vegas. This was a massive gathering of the top RE/MAX people from across the globe. The energy was electric. While at dinner in the ballroom, I discovered that my American RE/MAX counterparts at the table were using a different compensation plan for their Realtors, including larger commissions. My own system in New Zealand was a little dated by American standards. I listened to these other real estate leaders as they explained the standards they used. I made a decision before dinner was even concluded to revamp the compensation plan for my agents. Within a month, we were using it.

As a leader, I can make those strong decisions. That is the kind of "breaking the rules" I mean. Be a risk-taker. Try new things. Think outside the box. Accept those challenges.

To a point.

There are other rules—whether they are the legalities of real estate transactions or moral rules that should not be crossed—that should not be broken. Ethics is not an area you can compromise on and hope to be successful.

You may get away with an ethical lapse. Once.

That emboldens you, so you do it again. Then you may commit a bigger ethical lapse. And before you know it, your career and reputation will be in tatters.

I once met a gentleman who was the chief financial officer for a well-known international nonprofit. We were talking about ethics in finances, and I asked him, genuinely curious, how it is people embezzle, and think they won't be caught.

He responded:

"The ethical lapse usually starts small. A person who writes the checks or works in accounting 'borrows' a little bit of money because they cannot make their bills that month. They intend to pay it right back. But they can't right away because, after all, they're already behind on their bills, and they got away with it once. So, they do it again—small still. Eventually, it escalates, they get bolder, and hopefully they are caught before they do too much damage."

We all love iconoclasts—those who break the rules. But we must maintain our moral code. Some rules are not to be broken. That is the only way to success.

CHAPTER 9

COMING FULL CIRCLE

ometimes on quiet mornings, before my kids have woken, I step outside and take in the view from my beautiful home on a clifftop in one of the most affluent suburbs in Auckland. If the wind is just right, and the clouds are few, I can see the water. I know my family is safe inside. I can hear the call of seabirds. I almost want to pinch myself.

This is my life.

And it's a great one!

How could a boy from a refugee camp rise to this level?

After thirty years of being in real estate, working hard, I achieved goals beyond my childhood imagination now. When I was nineteen, I always envisioned that I would one day have a company and employ people and help my community.

I can remember going through a fast-food restaurant drive-through and seeing what felt like fifty staff members and thinking, *Wow, this franchise is employing so many people. Someday that will be me.*

Today, my company provides employment for over three hundred people.

I used to read about companies with $50 million in sales. Or even $100 million. I thought that was the height of success.

But today I have a company with over a billion dollars in sales.

Starting out in real estate, I admired real estate companies that had five or six offices in one suburb. *That* was success.

I now have a company that owns RE/MAX for the entire *country* of New Zealand. I have an office in almost every town, and we are still growing. Every eight hours, someone in my company has sold a piece of real estate, sometimes two or three in that time frame.

As my thinking got bigger and I stopped limiting the size of my ambitions, I wanted to go international.

As of this writing, I now own RE/MAX New Zealand and Fiji. The reach of my visions is still expanding.

From a refugee arriving to New Zealand having no family there, not knowing a soul, not speaking English, needing the support of a church sponsor to today—if I put it in a novel, some people might not believe it.

Some people might look at my journey and think it is impossible. And it might be if you approach it incorrectly. You have to invest in people first. Most people invest in a company, and then they take the money out. And that may be fine for a while, but it is not sustainable. I have always used my money to invest in infrastructure and training and developing people. When you develop people, they can talk like you, think like you. They can troubleshoot. Then there's not just *one* of you anymore. There are *five* of you. You are replicating the pathway to success over and over.

The Elephant and the Dog

A dog came to the elephant and said, "Hey, Elephant, in two years I have produced three litters of pups. And in those two years, you produced only one baby. What's wrong with you?"

The elephant then said, "Well, the difference between you and me is when my baby arrives, it weighs two hundred pounds, it trembles the earth, and it looks so magnificent that everyone takes photos of my babies. And your babies, all they do is bark."

I see a lot of people in business who bark and make a lot of noise—"Oh, I did this, I did that. I achieved so much and I spent so much. I got this luxury car" and so on. When the market turns, they lose these trappings of wealth. And here I am, the elephant, still being quiet, quiet, and next minute, boom, RE/MAX Fiji. I am the elephant who achieved. Now, I'm here achieving my ultimate dream of my very own book published by Forbes worldwide.

Don't be like the dog and chase your tail with useless activity. Be the patient elephant, and develop your beautiful baby who makes the earth tremble.

A Journey to the Ancestors

I don't know that I understood what a maelstrom of feelings this writing would stir as I revisited my life from the moment of fleeing Vietnam to today. This process has been a time for introspection—and a time for deep gratitude.

Very few of us are lucky enough to come full circle. I am one of the fortunate few. I could see my journey so clearly as I wrote. How had I gone from a penniless boy to a millionaire? But how, also, had I traveled round the circle of life to achieve wisdom?

In the thirty-seven years since my family left Vietnam, I've been back twice. Once for business and once with my family, including my children. One of the things our family did while there was to visit our ancestors' graves. I told my wife and children the stories I knew about our small village and about the generations before me and before my kids.

Our ancestors' resting place is atop a very tall mountain whose peak appears to touch the clouds. To reach it, we had to trek through steamy overgrowth and jungle. The journey up was arduous, even with a worn path to the top. The sun beat down on us the whole way, humidity so thick that the air felt wet, and palm fronds occasionally scratching at us along the path or whacking us in the face.

My children did not complain; I was proud of them. I had hoped that they, too, would understand, at least a little, what this trip meant. These were their ancestors too. Periodically, as we hiked, we'd stop and rest, sipping water and mentally and physically preparing for the next uphill stretch. As we approached the top, the climb grew steeper, the vegetation still thick. We were sweating and hungry, but it was a pilgrimage. The legend is the tougher the climb, the more blessings your ancestors bestow on you. The difficult climb demonstrates the respect you are offering to your family's generations who came before you.

At last, we emerged at the top. From there, we could see for miles in every direction. I could not help but think that this was a beautiful and honorable resting place for our ancestors—a place where they were closer to the sky.

We bowed and left offerings, and we recited prayers. For me, it was very emotional. I am not sure I expected to be so moved because, after all, I had left as a child. I imagined whispering to them, *Look, Ancestors, look at what your familial line has become. Your sacrifices have brought me here, full circle. I have achieved far beyond what anyone could have imagined in our war-torn country. You may rest in peace, knowing I am providing for my own family and our extended family. I am honoring my parents, as well as my elders. I am honoring you by coming here.*

My children and wife were quiet and reverent. I think they understood that I was absorbing the remarkableness of this moment.

We all have memories, but some we cannot access. For example, while I could remember my own and my parents' and siblings' lives before we left Vietnam, as well as the experiences we had as refugees, because I was young when we left, not everything was a crystal clear memory—they were hazy with time.

However, the human brain is a remarkable organ. There in Vietnam, in the sights, sounds, and heat of the jungle and the mountaintop, a visceral feeling came to me. It was as if I were back in my childhood. It all became so clear to me, so vivid. The thick, humid air, the very scent of the soil and the jungle and the mountaintop, the cackling birds and occasional rustling of the wind through the trees, all evoked rich recollections.

My family, after paying their respects, stood further away from me and allowed me some quiet time with my ancestors. I was humbled by visiting this sacred place.

After our hike to their resting place, the next day we spent time with my aunt. She had not seen me since we left Vietnam, and I had been excited to see her. But our culture is very funny (and perhaps like your own culture and traditions). It doesn't matter how long you haven't seen someone; if they're your auntie, they're still going to give you a piece of their mind and tell you what to do. They still hold that familial power hierarchy over you, which is special. They are your elders. I was secretly amused and warmed by her connection to me, even after all that time.

Grab at Your Opportunities

My other full circle moment was when an important billionaire from Vietnam flew to New Zealand and asked to meet with me about potentially doing business with him. He was in Wellington, however, which is an eight-hour drive or a one-hour flight from where I live. I had a conference the next day, and I thought there was just too much going on to connect with him. Yet, perhaps because he was from Vietnam, and also because I have learned to grab at opportunities, I decided to try to make it work. I listened to my instincts and my own advice to take advantage of every chance for success that comes your way.

After all, I realized if he came all the way from Vietnam to New Zealand, and he had this small window to discuss investment and perhaps our working together, I needed to seize the opportunity. I quickly made the decision to spend $800 on a flight to go and meet him along with one of my colleagues in Wellington.

My real estate colleague picked me up from the airport. We went straight to the billionaire's hotel, picked him up, and drove to meet some consultants for about forty-five minutes. When that meeting ended, the investor said, "I need to go to the airport now, because I am flying on to Australia."

I had barely met this man. Still, I said, "Well, I'll come to the airport with you—it will give us more of a chance to talk." I understood, with the potential for business, this connection meant that this time together was not to be missed. This man owns sixty-five companies, employing 26,500 staff. He is one of the biggest developers in Vietnam, and I was incredibly impressed at what he was doing there—at what the entire country was doing, evolving into a sophisticated cultural mecca. It excited me, and I wondered if my ancestors were facilitating this meeting! He was two years older than I, and he gave me his brochures and more information on his company. He asked me many questions about my own background.

I knew his next flight was to talk to a different Realtor in Australia. However, to me, this was both about business and, once again, about taking an interest in someone and their story and background.

At his gate, we sat together, which added another thirty minutes with him. I bought us each a sandwich. It kind of amused me that no matter how much money we have, just like the idea that we all put on our pants one leg at a time, we all have to eat. Airport sandwiches or thick steaks and lobster tails—we all can share a meal.

With our connection solidified, he invited me to Vietnam to meet with him and learn more about his company, which I happily accepted.

Had I not decided to grab at that opportunity, the relationship would not have developed. This is a lesson that you go at any cost to meet someone who's got higher power or levels of influence than you because the opportunity may never come again. It's fate. Grab onto its tail!

A few days later, I was invited to meet the General Assembly of Vietnam officially while their delegation was in New Zealand. I marveled at the ways in which Vietnam was now intersecting with my life.

My brother and I were told we needed to dress up and appear at the delegation's hotel, the magnificent five-star Cordis hotel in Auckland. When we arrived at the hotel, there were bodyguards, as well as people lining up to meet with the foreign dignitaries. When I went in the room, it felt like a kingdom—a magnificent suite. Six or seven reporters were going *click, click, click, click* with paparazzi-like cameras nonstop. I saw a few stars from the flashes going off.

Video cameras were also recording our entire conversation. I told them about the global reputation of RE/MAX and how we could help their country both in Vietnam and in investments throughout the globe. Afterward, I discovered the handshake I had with this leader of the General Assembly of Vietnam (the third most important leader in their country) made all of the Vietnamese news channels and newspapers. My success as a "native son" of Vietnam in New Zealand was of interest.

Rise

From being penniless to being a millionaire many times over. From a refugee to a citizen. From fleeing Vietnam to reconnecting to it in a powerful way, recognizing my ancestors and their sacrifices. I can only give thanks.

The national flower of Vietnam is the lotus. It is said that it reaches through the mud and the murky water of ponds to emerge and show off its power and beauty to the world—its strength. I think of the watercress I harvested in New Zealand. Watercress also grows in the mud, and the murk yet provides rich nutrition for people.

Refugee camps the world over are places where the poorest people are treated like so much mud. Yet so many of us bloom where we are planted. We learn the value of hard work, determination, and resiliency and to rise above our circumstances.

I have come full circle. I have risen from the mud. I have achieved what some only dream about—exponential success. And I am not finished yet!

I urge you to rise as well. Take these success principles, and apply them to your own life and career. I know I will only keep growing, keep challenging myself, and, most importantly, showing others that they too can rise above any circumstances to become anything they desire. You can. Believe it, and embrace the art of exponential success.